Making Pearls
From Grit

I Aitken

For Christina Lang Aitken and Doreen White Chapman

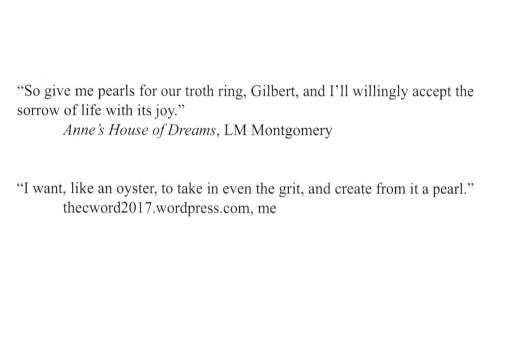

"So give me pearls for our troth ring, Gilbert, and I'll willingly accept the sorrow of life with its joy."
Anne's House of Dreams, LM Montgomery

"I want, like an oyster, to take in even the grit, and create from it a pearl."
thecword2017.wordpress.com, me

CONTENTS

The Dimple

It wasn't the lump, because that seemed hardly noticeable, and certainly neither husband nor I thought it anything other than one of those fatty lumps that surfaces and disappears throughout the menstrual cycle.

It was the dimple.

And even though the lump didn't disappear, neither did it seem to grow. I paid it no attention. But the dimple grew in width and, suddenly, depth. I glanced at it often; down at it, when in the shower. But never, I think, at its reflection. Never face on in the mirror. Not that I recall. Which is odd, because I frequently invest time in surveying all the many faults of my face and body, especially since having children. I am fascinated and appalled by my brutalised, battered, post-breastfeeding boobs, and the rolls of fat and pitted skin of my overstretched stomach.

Nevertheless, the dimple was overlooked for some months.

And then suddenly, one morning, it dawned on me that a dimple as large as this one was not normal. Retrospect has given me the clarity of thought to realise that I had been in denial. I didn't want the dimple to be anything dubious, so I pretended it wasn't. But finally I thought it had reached a size that merited drawing it to someone else's attention. I drew it to husband's.

At this point you might be wondering why husband wouldn't already have noticed it or, having noticed it, not mentioned it in passing. And that's a very good question. It's not as though we don't have, you know… an intimate aspect of our relationship.

But I can't tell you why he might not have noticed it, because I don't know – more to the point, I don't want to ask him. If I questioned him on his observational skills, I worry that he would somehow feel to blame. And blame is very much an action that should have no part in a cancer diagnosis.

Anyway – husband seemed unconcerned. Husband seemed unsurprised.

Husband suggested I see a GP. "But we're going to Japan on Monday, so what's the point?" I asked.

Ah yes, Japan.

At this point I need to explain that we were intending to go to Japan for 11 weeks. Why? Because of husband's midlife crisis, that's why. Husband does not argue with this diagnosis, even though I can only guess at it, since husband is one of those popular breeds of men who does not speak of his emotions. Suffice to say, this personal, predictable and terribly stereotypical predicament, rather than manifesting itself in a mistress or a Porsche, surfaced in a sudden desire to go and work in a Japanese associate's Tokyo office for a short period. I had, for a while, ignored his occasional comments on the existence of this office, and the possibility of his visiting it; after several of these comments, I finally cottoned on.

> Husband: A Japanese associate says if we ever
> want to go to Tokyo, he has space in his office I
> could work in.
> Me: That's nice.
> [One month later]
> Husband: There's that Japanese associate saying
> I could work in his office if we ever want to go to
> Tokyo.
> Me: Yes.
> [One month later]
> Husband: Would it be a possibility, going to
> Tokyo, do you think? Just for a couple of months,
> or something? Only, my Japanese associate says I
> could work in his office.
> Me, thinking: *Ahhh, he wants to go to Tokyo.*

To cut a long story short – skip to the end!* – we had arranged an 11-week trip to Japan, taking our children with us. And this trip was to start in four days' time. What was the point, I asked husband, of seeing the

---

* This is one of my favourite lines from Noughties sitcom series *Spaced*, starring Jessica Stevenson and Simon Pegg. Not at all relevant in this context

GP now? He reasoned that at least I could get some peace of mind from her, whatever the diagnosis. Otherwise I would spend 11 weeks in Japan worrying about this dimple. So the appointment was made.

Retrospect has given me the ability to say that just the look on the GP's face confirmed the diagnosis I feared it would be. Which is hugely unfair on her professional abilities, since she did to a large extent remain poker-faced and unforthcoming. Memory is a fickle and misleading thing – I may now be claiming a comprehension I didn't actually have at the time. Hindsight, and all that.

Having undressed my top half, I lay under her distant scrutiny (distant as in objective; she wasn't the other side of the room or anything. That would have been ineffective); she said she couldn't make a definitive diagnosis, and it could be nothing – it was usually nothing – but that she would like to refer me. "But I'm going to Japan on Monday," I blurted. (As far as my subconscious was concerned, she had basically confirmed what I already feared. But we had this trip to Eastern Asia planned and ready to put into full execution. It didn't even enter my head that the trip be abandoned – so much had gone into the preparations, and it would cost money, time and possibly husband's sanity to cancel. I wouldn't put him through that.)

There followed a silent dialogue between me and the GP; she standing with pursed lips and a thoughtful frown, me with an incompetent, helpless expression.

> GP, (probably) thinking: *Hmm. Well, that's awkward.*
> Me, thinking: *I know, I'm a twit. I shouldn't have left it till now.*
> GP, (probably) thinking: *You maybe shouldn't have left it till now. What to do…?*
> Me, thinking: *Come on, you're a doctor. You can do anything. Solve this please!*

"Why don't you see a doctor in Tokyo?" asked my GP, with such a wonderful degree of nonchalance, I felt slightly ashamed I hadn't thought of that. "I'm sure they're more than capable," the GP added, with a shrug of her shoulders. "In the meantime I'll refer you here anyway, so you're in the system."

It was with a perhaps misplaced sense of relief that I returned home. "She doesn't really know what's causing it so said she'd refer me," I told husband. "But she also said I should see a doctor in Japan. So let's just go ahead with the trip and deal with it when we're out there."

It was that simple.

Chapter One

I f you were of a superstitious disposition, you might think that the opening blurb on the home page of my travel blog[1] about our trip to Eastern Asia was asking for trouble: "A Scottish family let loose in Japan for 11 weeks… What could possibly go wrong?"

I started writing the blog a good month before that suggestive dimple appeared; two months before we set off on our travels; and two and a half months before my diagnosis. I distinctly remember husband expressing a cautious "Hmmm," when he read those lines, his tone loaded with an uncharacteristic superstition.

The thing is, I don't feel that anything did go wrong. We ended up spending five and a half weeks in Asia, rather than the originally planned 11; but it was five and a half weeks of adventure, education, entertainment, pleasure and enlightenment, interspersed with the occasional medical appointment at which unpleasant news was broken.

I can't say, however, that my experience of the Japanese healthcare system was anything other than great – not a recommended tourist destination but if you do end up there, don't worry, you'll have a splendid time.

I have never thought myself particularly good at compartmentalising my thoughts. If something is bothering me, the stress of that seeps into every crevice of my mind, tainting all other thoughts. But in those few days after I saw the GP, I barely thought of what a referral implied, or of what I should perhaps be afraid of. First, we were too busy to be anxious. And second, floating around in my subconscious was that old edict: if there's something you can do about a problem, why worry; and if there's nothing you can do, there's no point worrying. In other words, I would cross the Japanese doctor's diagnosis bridge when I came to it.

The very next day husband and I attended the funeral of the wife of one of his childhood friends. She was young, and a mother, and while I couldn't sing the hymns because I was choking over the music and the words, all I could think as I gazed across the chapel at her two children, cwtched into their daddy, was how unfair it all was. How utterly miserable.

And then those tears and any thoughts of my own predicament were swept away, by a weekend of cleaning, tidying and packing. There is a lot of administration involved when you're upping sticks for longer than the usual two-week summer holiday.

I had researched decongestants for the flight, and which medicines we would be allowed to take into Japan (as noted on the foreign travel advice page of the UK government's website, Japan has very strict drug laws and won't allow into the country medicines such as Vicks inhalers, or those for allergies and sinus problems, cold and flu medication containing Pseudoephedrine, or over-the-counter painkillers containing codeine. "Foreign nationals have been detained and deported for offences – ignorance may not be considered a defence [2]."); I had also researched English-speaking doctors, with that maternal fear in the back of my mind that one of the children might have an accident or fall ill and I should have the details of a medic ready and close at hand; put together a home-learning plan (since we had decided not to have a private tutor and couldn't afford to place the children into an international school); practised, cried over and marvelled at the Japanese language and hiragana (one of its three character sets[3]); cleaned and tidied the house to such an extent I discovered nooks and crannies of our home I didn't know existed; panicked about the sound of people eating noodle soup (I have misophonia*); selected which clothes to take and which to leave…

We would be having a family stay in our house while we were away, so in the previous weeks I had been gradually storing away items of sentiment or breakability, and rearranging those – kitchenware, toys and books – I was happy to see used. (Or, to be entirely honest, that I couldn't

---

*Misophonia is a condition that elicits anger or disgust when the sufferer hears someone, for example, sniffing, chewing, slurping, breathing…

be bothered to pack away. We own a lot of shit.)

The children were instructed to store away their most precious toys – son swept up most of his Lego models and solemnly packed them in boxes.

(Oh! Yes, there's a story about the boxes, too. I had gone online and ordered ten large boxes in which to parcel away our things. I am a little lackadaisical when it comes to checking price tags. Miraculously, however, when the company emailed me on the morning of delivery to confirm the order, I actually read the damn thing, and was slightly disconcerted when I saw this:

KL BROWN STRONGER ECONOBOX C125TT
508Lx508Wx508H PACK 20
QTY 10 PACK 20

Quantity 10; pack 20. Hmm. That must mean… wait, I'll do the maths… not my strong point, and I'm not confident I'm getting this but… 10 packs of 20 boxes… that's 200 boxes. I had ordered 200 boxes. And when I called the company to beg stupidity and ask them to cancel the order, the angelic lady on the other end of the phone (who was called Angela! Nominative determinism!) asked me if I hadn't seen the amount of money that would have come off my credit card. No, I said. I hadn't. Because as far as I was aware, I had ordered 10 boxes, and I knew how much that would be so why would I check the bill at the end? If I had noticed the £300 figure, sure, I might have realised more quickly the mistake I had made. Anyway, she got the pallets off the lorry and reimbursed my credit card, and we ended up with just 20 boxes, which turned out to be the perfect number.)

And those last two days at home were spent packing suitcases, bagging up the dirty laundry to store in the attic (I've had a sudden thought – is the laundry still up there? In the attic?), locating passports, buying enough cat food to last three months…

Suddenly the trip was real. It was so real, there was no room in my mind to process any information other than that related to flying 5735 miles across the world and living in a culture and society utterly unknown to me. It was so real that joining some friends for dinner two nights before we left, I found it difficult to engage in conversation, to extract myself from the logistical turmoil that engulfed my brain.

And then everything was done. All boxes ticked. I looked at husband and said, "This is going to be incredible," because I knew it would be. And he looked relieved.

We didn't do a lot of flying, as a family. In recent years it had been such a rare occurrence for me that I had forgotten all the rules of flying – the security etiquette – such as placing liquids in clear bags. I knew I couldn't have a knife or gun in my hand luggage, but I don't tend to carry those anyway, so it wasn't a problem. I must have been somewhat overcome by excitement, because as we approached security at Edinburgh Airport, and were putting our hand luggage on the conveyor belts, husband called out and asked if I had my laptop in my bag. "Yes," I replied, not understanding why he asked. "And my Kindle and iPad."

"Those aren't supposed to be in there," said husband, but not, in my opinion, vociferously enough. I shrugged, and put my bag through the x-ray machine.

Oh, how I regretted that shrug.

I walked past the x-ray machine to the security woman, who was in the middle of berating another traveller for failing to remove her tray from the counter and put it away. She was abrupt enough for Tray Lady to exclaim, "Rude!" as she glanced at me in search of some sympathy. I smiled serenely.

My bag trundled out of the x-ray machine onto a belt behind the security woman. She hauled it off and asked me, "Any electrical goods in here?"

Oh. Um. "My laptop. And Kindle and iPad," I said foolishly.

"Take them out," she commanded. "Those should have gone in a separate tray."

I removed the offending articles, and she placed them in different trays before returning them to start their journey again. They rejoined me at the bottom of the legitimate conveyor belt but when my bag reappeared, it was again on the conveyor belt of doom.

"You got any liquids in there?" asked the security woman.

Liquids? Of course not. Why would I have liquids in my bag?

The security woman opened the bag and pulled out, in quick succession, bottles of Calpol, Karvol and Olbas Oil*, remarking "What's this?" as she extracted each one.

Liquids, I guess.

"They need to be put in a see-through bag," she said, putting them each in a see-through bag and exiling them to separate trays, to begin again their x-ray journey. At this point I suddenly remembered all the new-fangled airport security measures**, such as taking all your electrical goods out your hand luggage, and putting small bottles of liquids in transparent bags. Too late now, though, isn't it doll face? You've brazenly attempted to break the rules and are now holding everyone up, ruining the security woman's already stressful day and making a dick of yourself.

And yet again, despite the liquids having been removed, my hand luggage was expelled from the x-ray machine onto the conveyor belt of doom. "What else have we got in there?" the security woman asked. I was suddenly overwhelmed by the desire to make a run for it and leave behind all my stuff. I wracked my brain to think of how many other illicit items were in my hand luggage. I was quite prepared to be arrested for stupidity.

"Nothing," I said.

"The machine definitely sees something," she said.

Then the machine is more intelligent than me, I thought miserably. By some miracle, I suddenly recollected my make-up bag, and suggested that my foundation might be the final recalcitrant item.

"Let's try that," said the security woman, who had been so much more patient with me than with the poor woman who forgot to put away her tray. Maybe the security woman thought this was a work assessment, and her employer had sent me in as a customer services exercise. *No-one could be this stupid*, she must have thought.

Finally, with the foundation removed, my bag and all its contents made their way down the approved luggage conveyor belt in five different trays. I gathered it all together – then put my trays away.

It was a 12-hour journey in total, flying via Amsterdam. It was a

* All perfectly innocent medical liquids, well known to any carers of germ-magnets. Aka children
** In place since 2001

journey I had prepared for by stashing away a supply of diazepam, aka Valium, since I have struggled in the past with being confined in a small space for any length of time. I only needed one wee 2mg pill to last me the entire journey, though, since it saw me giggling and high as a kite at Edinburgh airport, and then sink into an insensible lethargy on the plane, hypnotised by the drone of the engines and the warmth of the space.

The children were delighted by the plethora of films they could watch in the comfort of their seats, and were unable to sleep at all during the journey, the excitement and distractions far too overwhelming for relaxation. Landing at Narita Airport, son, who had been having karate lessons for five years and was highly enamoured of all things Japanese, was elated. He behaved as though he had finally come home, announcing his love of everything he saw, from the aeroplanes and buildings to the rice balls and fire engines.

He bowed and said, "Arigato gozaimasu*," to every official he passed as we wended our way through the airport, which seemed to delight those who were on the receiving end of his gratitude. Son was in his element, and remained so for the rest of our stay in Eastern Asia.

The train journey from Narita Airport to Tokyo was fascinating enough to cut through our exhaustion and encroaching jet lag. The buildings were so very different, the sky so very sharply blue... I was fascinated by a screen at the end of our carriage which showed details of the train service. Japan is noted for its reliably punctual train service, so I was interested to see that, actually, several other trains were delayed, and for the following reasons (as stated, word for word, in English, on the screen):
1 Wind
2 Injured person
3 Obstacle thing.

The entire journey was gratifyingly smooth. We found our AirBnB apartment, and were delighted by its size, its facilities, its location... (Apart from the fact that it was next to a train line. Right next to it. Like, this close to it. And not just the train line, but also the level crossing,

* Thank you

whose warning sound to pedestrians and drivers was a persistent BOING BOING BOING BOING BOING. I was not best pleased.) The children each chose their room and immediately started unpacking their suitcases and making themselves at home... Oh! Yes, it was a three-bedroom apartment. Who knew? I totally thought we would be staying in a shoebox. But this place not only had three bedrooms, it also had four balconies, a utility room and a walk-in wet room. It also had lots of jars of oils, sauces and pickles in the kitchen, since one regular tenant was a chef, who taught cookery in the apartment.

Once the excitement had dissipated a little, and we had explored the flat, I was able to sit down and check my emails.

And I had received a message from the Run For The Cure Foundation[4], (a Japanese charity helping to reduce breast cancer through education, screening, and treatment). My paranoid-mum researches on English-speaking doctors had taken me to a site which, the day after my UK GP appointment, I scoured for any information on breast cancer specialists. There was a lot of information to wade through. Too much. So many doctors, how was I to choose one? And then, thank god, this charity popped up, and I thought, well, if it's a breast cancer charity, maybe it can help.

And my desperate message to them via their site was answered just a few days later.

"There are more than a few hospitals offering breast cancer screening in Tokyo; but St Luke's International Hospital may be the best one to make an appointment and visit as the hospital offers full English-serviced patient care."

English-serviced! Well, thank goodness for that. What did English-serviced mean? I didn't care. This wonderful woman had offered me a lifeline, some inside information on where to go for medical attention.

But I didn't make the call, not immediately. We were to stay only one night in our Tokyo apartment, before heading off the very next morning to Hokkaido, the northernmost Japanese prefecture[5] and island, where we were to sample the Sapporo Snow Festival, smell the sulphurous mountains of Noboribetsu and suffer the pancake-thieving magpies of Hakodate (well, only son suffered those, although it was traumatic enough to threaten to overshadow much of the holiday).

I thought that if I called the hospital to make an appointment, and then said, oh but I can't make an appointment for the next week, it would sound a bit silly. So we set off on our mini-tour of the north while I safely shelved the contact details of the hospital. Just knowing I had the number, and somewhere to go when we got back from Hokkaido, put my mind at rest.

We spent the next four nights force-feeding ourselves this new culture, gobbling it up, taking in the astonishingly diverse sights and smells of this country. So much stimulation, so much sensory information…

…The soft ethereal snow of Sapporo ("The powder there is supposed to be amazing," a friend back home had said, and it had taken me a moment to remember that she is an avid skier, and was talking about snow, not cocaine), and the incredibly detailed ice and snow sculptures of the festival (a life-sized Arc de Triomphe, a gigantic R2-D2…). Equally impressive was the way in which the crowds were gently shepherded to walk around, up and down the 1.5km avenue of sculptures in an anti-clockwise fashion. All very orderly…

…The opportunity to put into use just a fraction of the masses of Japanese we had learned in the run-up to this trip – a crash course in the language, for three hours a week for three months, though I'm afraid all I got was the wrong end of the stick when a lovely senior citizen on the train pointed to a leaflet about the Snow World amusement park, failing to infer that all she wanted to know was whether we were going there, leading to me repeating, "Watashi wa Sukottorando-jin desu[*]." I'm sure she didn't care what nationality we were, although she did respond by saying, "Whisky! Sapporo whisky[**]!" And that was the only point at which we could identify with one another and share a common (one hesitates to say) interest, since after that we fell into an embarrassed silence and looked out different windows…

...The impression that there was no such thing as unemployment in Japan, since absolutely everybody seemed to have a job, no matter how small. Two men would wave cars into and out of a car-park, and

---

[*] "I am Scottish"
[**] "Sapporo" whisky is the Nikka brand, whose distilleries are actually in Yoichi, 58km west of Sapporo. Probably more famous in the West is Sapporo beer…

then wave pedestrians across the entrance to the car-park; someone would walk behind a reversing lorry, notifying everybody of the lorry's movements by way of a whistle and flag, despite the fact the lorry was also beeping; at museums, someone to direct you to the ticket office, someone to sell you a ticket, someone to check the ticket, then someone to greet you as you enter…

…The many types of slipper, along with the etiquette that dictated which slipper you could wear in which room. This was delightfully complicated. In our Sapporo hotel we were provided with slippers, though we were allowed to wear shoes in our room, and were not allowed to wear the slippers in the restaurant; in the Noboribetsu hotel (which was of a more traditional set-up), you were provided with two pairs of slippers, one of which you had to wear in your room, the other you could wear in the restaurant and spa. You could also wear your spa pyjamas in the restaurant; and in the Hakodate hotel, slippers were provided but their use wasn't enforced and they didn't seem to care what you wore where.

We left Hakodate and returned to Tokyo on the Shinkansen*, a smooth and efficient journey which was made slightly more interesting by the fact that husband had suffered a serious bout of food poisoning the night before, and I was genuinely intrigued about how he would cope on the four-hour train journey; also, we were all seated on different rows of the train, one behind the other, thanks to husband booking tickets at the last minute. Behind me sat daughter, sandwiched between two Japanese men and watching a succession of films on her tablet, apparently unfazed by the experience; an assumption that was swiftly quashed when we arrived in Tokyo and she wailed, "I hate Japan, I miss home, I don't want to be here any more, I want to go home!"

According to my diary, I left it another day before I called St Luke's International Hospital to make an appointment there, but I have no idea why. While husband went to work, I and the children went to Yoyogi Park[6], where we watched other visitors offering their thanks and prayers at the Meiji Shrine. I seem to have been far too laidback about the whole

---

* bullet train

breast dimple affair. Either laidback or in denial.

No, not in denial. I've known since I was 30 that I would get breast cancer. My paternal grandmother died of it at 39. My aunt and mum both had it, though they were in their sixties, and survived. I mean, come on, what were the chances? Surely pretty high?

Since the lady from Run For The Cure had referred to St Luke's as a "fully English-serviced" hospital, I expected whoever answered the phone to do so in English. Lol. When, a couple of days later, I did make the call, I was answered by a stream of Japanese, which took me something by surprise, though I was able to chant the now daily litany of "Eigo o hanasemasuka*?" This, too, was answered by another stream of Japanese, but fortunately I didn't panic and hang up, since only a few seconds later another voice came on the line, saying, "Good morning and thank you for calling. This is the translation service. How can I help you?"

I was so relieved by this, I didn't give a fig about whether he was a doctor or not, and if my predicament might embarrass him – I didn't hold back from explaining my symptoms and situation, and as good as begged for help.

It was suggested that I would need to have a mammogram, and so an appointment to see a breast specialist was booked for two days later.

In Tokyo I took the children in search of a playpark. We had found two glorious "parks", vast in scale, and imbued with a tranquility provided by birds, manicured plants and gardens, neat avenues of trees… But no swings or slides.

We wended our way north-west of the apartment, in a direction we had not been before, through the residential streets, across a very busy road near Shinjuku and finally, hurrah, into a park (Shinjuku Chuo) with a very exciting looking climbing frame and slide.

Alas, daughter was soon reduced to tears by the tape that surrounded it to keep children out. A quick email to our Japanese teacher provided a translation of the sign on the tape:

"As a result of an inspection, something dangerous was found. As it is dangerous, please do not use."

* Do you speak English?

The children consoled themselves with an ice-cream and a very wide, very slippery concrete slide which they ran up and down 70 times. I stood watching them, entranced by the peace of this square in among high-rise offices and flats; also the musicians who, barred from rehearsing in their homes for fear of upsetting the neighbours, routinely practise their instruments in the parks of the city. A man playing sax sat near the bottom of the slide, and the children's whoops and rapid descents were accompanied by gentle jazz. Further on in the park, standing in the centre of a small bandstand, was a violinist who nodded to passersby.

It was a peaceful day.

And then this day was over and it was time to go to the clinic.

Did I feel nervous? Was I anxious about what was to come? I knew what mammograms were like, since I had had two before. I must have assumed it would be much the same process, and I don't recall being particularly concerned. I shepherded the children as we, inattentive to our surroundings, followed husband, who was navigating us around the public transport system. I think there was a little confusion as to which of the many subway exits we needed for the clinic, but eventually we surfaced, crossed a road, weaved through some skyscrapers and found ourselves at the entrance to what looked like an office block.

The clinic reception was more redolent of a spa. Two beautiful young women sat at the counter, and the armchairs in the bright, airy waiting area were deep and cushioned. "Eigo o…" I began, but was swiftly interrupted by one of the beautiful young women.

"Yes, do you have an ID number?" Stumbling block number one, I thought, but when I explained I was a first-time patient – I almost said guest – I was given four forms to fill out. I sat down and urged husband to take the children away somewhere for entertainment. I would call him when I was finished. (Finished what? I didn't know.)

As I waded through the forms, the receptionist became increasingly nervous that I risked being late for my appointment. I smiled in appeasement. "Nearly finished!" I said. She handed me my new ID card and told me to keep it for all future appointments.

And then I was ushered through into a changing room, where I was asked to change into a kimono and slippers, placing my belongings in a locker. It was almost as though I was about to have a massage, it was all so serene, and quiet, and gentle.

And I didn't feel totally self-conscious when I sat on a chair in the hall, in my huge kimono and slippers, and noticed that nobody else was. Wearing a kimono and slippers. They were all in their civvies. They didn't stare, anyway.

The mammogram was surprisingly rough. The practitioner, muttering "sumimasen*" and "may I?", pushed and pulled me around on the plate, squeezing the life out of my breasts, making me almost breathless with the bruised pain.

"Does it hurt?" asked the practitioner, "Is it painful?" *Yes, of course it is*, I thought. *But I've had babies, so it's all relative.* I laughed breezily and shook my head.

Mammogram finished, I was guided back out and seated in the hall. Classical music was piped tinnily into the room, and I sat for 15 mind-numbing, lonely minutes before being taken into another room for an ultrasound scan.

It was during this scan that my assumptions and fears were finally confirmed, though the practitioner, having little English and clearly not thinking it her place to say anything, said nothing. Twenty minutes I was on that bed. Twenty minutes, as she placed gel on my chest and ran the probe over and over my breast, a couple of times the left one, but over and over the right, clicking on the computer keyboard, zooming in on certain sections of the image and highlighting it, zooming out, zooming in on another section and highlighting it.

I lay staring at the ceiling, occasionally glancing sideways at the computer screen to translate whatever it was that she saw there. I saw nothing but a wash of grey shades. The ceiling gave no reassurances, offered no distractions. Its blankness was a canvas on which my imagination drew concerns and fears; my stomach churned as I fought to lie still.

After 20 minutes, she indicated to me that I should stay where I was and left the room. She was gone for 10 minutes. I continued lying staring at the

* Excuse me

ceiling, unsure what to think. There was definitely a problem – that much was clear from the practitioner's assiduous scanning. I was miles from home, from all that I knew, and felt really quite detached from my body. That was now a slab of meat, which the practitioner understood better than I did. I had my suspicions but when would they tell me? *How* would they tell me?

And then the practitioner returned and took me out to the waiting area, saying, "Dr K will come and speak to you."

Another 15-minute wait, during which another woman entered and, after a short time, left the office in front of me, bowing as she backed out the door, repeating, "Domo arigato onegaishimasu, domo arigato sensei*." And then Dr K – sensei – appeared at the door and beckoned me into her room.

I entered and sat down.

"See your mammogram here? And your ultrasound here?" she pointed to images on her computer screen and I stared at them, fathoming nothing from either. "There is a shadow in your right breast," she said. "It is breast cancer."

I knew this, of course. But there was a part of my mind wondering how she could be this certain just from some pictures. I sat looking at her and nodding, waiting for the solution.

"There is shadows in your left breast but that is nothing," Dr K shrugged. She continued explaining the diagnosis but I didn't hear a word because I became fixated on the way she slow-blinked as she worked her way through a sentence. It seemed to be a nervous tic but I didn't know whether it was because she was picking through her knowledge of the English language or because she felt uneasy breaking this news to a foreign woman. Or, indeed, breaking this news full stop.

"I will refer you to main hospital," she continued. "You will have… biopsy?"

"Yes, a biopsy," I nodded helpfully.

"Yes, a needle biopsy, and we will know more. Take your information to the reception desk and they will…" she waved her hand, allowing me to

---

* "Thank you very much, many thanks teacher" – formal

17

finish the sentence in my head. *They will deal with it.*

At reception, a bill was printed and handed to me to pay immediately. I handed over a credit card, and waited for further instructions. None came.

"Umm… I think I'm supposed to be going to the other hospital… Will you make the appointment or should I?"

"You call this number," said the receptionist, handing me a card, "and tell them Dr K refers you. Tell them your ID number. They will do it."

When I had left the clinic and got the lift down to the ground floor lobby, I found a quiet corner and phoned husband.

"Where are you?" I asked.

"Dome City[7]."

"Okay. I've got breast cancer."

"Sorry, I didn't catch that…?"

"I've got breast cancer. The doctor just told me."

"Okay, do you want us to come back and get you?" Husband's level tone reflected my own.

"No, you stay there. I'll come and find you."

And off I went. If this had been London, where I lived for eight years, or even the streets of my current home town, my knowledge of the route would have afforded me the luxury of contemplation. But since this was Tokyo, and I didn't know where I was going, all my brain power was distracted and utilised for navigation.

It all went a bit Pete Tong.

The Tokyo train system is slightly complicated, in that each line is owned by a different train company, and it's usually necessary to buy a different ticket to travel on each line. I think. When with just the children I mostly used the Yamanote line, for which we needed only a Japan Rail pass, and which circled the city and took us pretty much every place we needed to be, from a station within walking distance of our apartment. When, as a family, we travelled further afield and used the other lines, husband invariably worked it all out and bought the tickets.

To this day I can't work out where I went wrong.

I knew I needed a ticket for the Mita Line, and having checked the price for my destination, I bought a ticket. That got me through the barrier, from where I followed signs for the Mita Line. Either a) the signs were wrong, or b) I misread them, or c) I didn't follow them correctly. I'm going for options b and c. Because I then walked for miles, down some stairs, along a platform, up some more stairs... and into another station concourse with more barriers. Barriers through which I definitely needed to go. Using the ticket I had already used to get through a barrier.

Obviously my ticket didn't work.

I turned and approached the ticket office, basically praying for a miracle of understanding.

"Eigo o hanasemasuka?" I asked.

"Sukotti," the man replied, unsmiling and thin-lipped. Sukotti? Scottish...? How did he know I was from Scotland? Okay, never mind. I proffered him the ticket and asked, "Mita line?"

He barely looked at it as he took it from my hand. "Not Mita line," he said dryly, before explaining in depth and at great length that the ticket I had bought was not valid for the Mita line. At least I think he did. It was all in Japanese so there could have been a few insults thrown in there too. For a moment I felt lost and slightly frightened, but while I stood like a rabbit caught in headlights, he took money from the till and gave it to me, repaying the difference between the ticket I had bought and the one I needed, and printed me out a new one[*].

Then he waved towards the barriers in vague boredom and I set off again, with no more mishaps. (And I realised he hadn't said "Sukotti", which doesn't mean anything, but "Sukoshi" – a little.)

Eventually I found Dome City, an amusement, shopping and dining park which assaults all five senses in one handy location. I located husband and children and as befitted that place and situation, merely hugged husband and confirmed what I'd told him on the phone. "I need to make an appointment for a biopsy," I said.

To escape the screams of the rollercoaster riders we went inside the Dome. I sat at the top of a flight of stairs in the centre of a department store and called St Luke's Hospital again.

---

[*] I'm sorry, can you imagine a British rail company employee doing that? Just paying back the money and printing a new ticket? Hell no. They'd have shaken their head and tutted, shouted loudly in English, printed out a new ticket and demanded full price, before handing out a three-page form to fill in and send off for reimbursement for the original ticket

"Eigo o hanasemasuka?" I asked the receptionist when she answered.

"Yes, of course," she said. "Do you have an ID number?"

Why yes, yes I did! This made me feel oddly prepared, and part of the system. As shoppers passed me on the stairs, glancing at me and then averting their eyes, I explained that I needed to make an appointment for a biopsy; one was made for the following week.

The call made, the appointment booked, husband and I took the children back outside to experience the fun of the fair. Daughter was treated to a pancake with ice cream, which impressed her so much she wrote about it in great detail in her diary when we got back to the apartment. I also took her on the log flume, a somewhat foolish decision, since we already knew that she has a fear of heights and a terror of the sensation of falling that comes with turbulent flights and, oh, I don't know, log flumes. She cried when we splashed to the bottom of the slope and berated me for taking her on the ride that she had begged to go on.

Husband took son on the rollercoaster, which I think he regretted, since, according to son, husband screamed like a baby. He denies this.

I didn't find it hard to switch off from the fact of my cancer. I didn't feel unwell. There was literally nothing more that could be done until I had the final, unarguable results of the biopsy. It was pointless worrying, and also almost impossible to do so, since we were surrounded by this whole new world, sights, sounds and experiences that enwrapped and enraptured me.

The next week was packed with visits to Ueno Zoo, notable for its incredibly voluble and opinionated flamingoes, and also the unlimited access to its pandas, unlike Edinburgh Zoo, where you have to join a waiting list to see the creatures; Kawazu, the town that usually sees Japan's first explosion of cherry blossom – or sakura – where we joined thousands of other blossom tourists meandering beneath the avenues of candy floss pink trees; an emergency homesickness-averting shopping trip, which took in the Disney Store and also Tokyo's Carnaby Street/Oxford Street hybrid, Takeshita Street, which sucked me and daughter in, swilled us around, flattened us and threw us out again; another trip back to Shinjuku Chuo, park of the taped-off climbing frame, which remained taped off; a jaunt to husband's office to take photos of the view from his windows, 22 floors up; and further exploration in search of a park, which we did find after we had spent half an hour immersing ourselves in a small garden of shrines, climbing the paths on a tiny hilly replica of Mount Fuji and taking deep breaths in the stillness.

And then it was the day of my biopsy.

I Aitken

The Blackout

I had never really had a problem with needles. While living and working in London, I started donating blood. My boss at the time was heading off to do his bit for society one lunchtime and suggested I join him. I thought it sounded like a virtuous way of supporting the NHS and injured souls, so I went along too.

I was squeamless* in those days. Didn't bat an eyelid during blood tests. But I must confess to some trepidation when the nurse approached with what was tantamount to a metal hosepipe, and stuck it in my arm. All went smoothly, however, and I was left with a wonderful smugness.

This self-satisfaction increased during the next couple of years, as I continued donating.

One morning, I made my contribution at a centre down the road from my office, before I headed into work. By this time, I felt like an old pro, and so when the obligatory pints of blood** had been extracted from my arm, I just walked out and up the road to the office. I needed to get to work. I honestly thought that since I was an old hand at this losing pints of blood malarkey, my body would be perfectly capable of functioning without the recommended tea and biscuits and a nice sit-down afterwards.

As I walked the short distance to my office, I became increasingly light-headed. By the time I got to work, the edges of my vision were going prickly and pixellated, and I felt weak at the knees. I sat down on some stairs in the lobby.

A security guard approached after a time and said, "You can't sit there."

"No, but I don't feel… great," I stammered. He shook his head and

* This isn't a word but will become one if this book is published
** It's actually 470ml, which is slightly less than one pint

stared at me. I stood.

Waiting at the lifts with a crowd of other miserable* workers, the edges of my vision became darker and I sank to the ground, lounging on the floor in a manner reminiscent of a 50s film star, though clearly not as alluring, since all the besuited employees ignored me. I mean, they blatantly wouldn't look at me. I, however, spotted a woman in the throng, and called out to her, "Could you help me to reception?" She looked surprised, but helped me up and supported me through to the lobby, where I sank onto an armchair and she left me.

The armchair, though, was not enough to bolster me. Merely having my head upright caused the world to go dark, and I slid to the ground again. Lying prone, my consciousness returned, and a couple of the office building managers came to assist me, though the receptionist scurried over to tell me, "You can't lie there!"

Enough anger fuelled me to lift my head and reply, "Where would you like me to faint?"

Each time I attempted to sit up, the lights switched off and I slumped to the floor again. An ambulance was called. Of course, when the paramedics arrived and were appraised of the situation, they diagnosed low blood pressure, caused by not having tea, biscuits and a nice sit-down after the blood donation. Very gradually, my blood pressure rose, and I was able to sit upright without blacking out, but they bundled me into a wheelchair, wheeled me out onto the London street thronged with rubbernecking passersby, loaded me into the ambulance and took me to Guy's Hospital anyway.

Since I wasn't an emergency, I sat in a cubicle alone for some time, feeling increasingly better as time went on. After having a sandwich, I discharged myself and got a taxi home. I didn't donate blood again after that because of the fear of fainting (and now I can't donate blood because of having had, you know, cancer), and the moral of this story is, you'll be fine if you just have tea, biscuits and a nice sit-down afterwards.

---

* They might have been perfectly happy, for all I know. Working for that particular employer, I'd be very surprised if they were

Chapter Two

I had never had a biopsy before. Of course I hadn't. Who's in the habit of having biopsies? It's not a regular thing for most people. So, what with the novelty and the memory of my last post-blood donation blackout in London, I was a bit nervous.

We set off that morning to travel by train to the main hospital the other side of Tokyo. At a pedestrian crossing outside our nearest station, waiting for the green man on the other side of the road was a middle-aged gentleman, grey hair, grey goatee, surrounded by what looked like a TV production crew: a photographer, a bloke with a proper video camera and another man holding the mic; and several other hangers-on.

"Someone famous," I said as coolly as I could, which was not very cool because I am a celebrity whore.

"Get your camera out," said husband. *No way*, I thought. *I don't want to look impressed.*

"No, you," I said.

We all stared at the apparent celeb. He glanced above our heads, laughed and waved. I turned round and saw some people hanging out their window, several floors up, waving excitedly.

He really was a celeb.

The green man lit up like a starting signal and I thrust my hand into my bag to retrieve my phone. Passing each other on the crossing I brazenly pointed the thing at him – he genially and generously waved the peace sign at me.

"Do you know who this chap is?" I messaged a pic to our Japan contact. "Since he was being followed by a film crew and waving at people, we assumed he's famous?"

"I don't watch TV much, but I knew his face," responded contact.

"My better half said 'Wow! He's very famous.'" It turned out to be a chap called Junji Takada[8], an actor and comedian. (He was born in 1947, which makes him rather more than middle-aged. I want whatever it is he's having.)

As we crossed the city by train and then on foot, traversing a bridge over the Sumida River, the day a dull grey which echoed across the clouds above and water below, I was somewhat distracted from thoughts of needles by the vastness of the Tokyo vistas, the height of the buildings and the constant rumbling traffic on the road over the bridge; and the odd sense of being so close to the ocean, despite not being able to see it. A sense of the river before us widening and reaching for the sea.

The hospital was as expected: clean, modern, busy, well signposted...

But when I tried to check in, I was asked for a referral letter I didn't have. I was briefly confused but then thought my ID card would solve everything. It didn't. I began to worry, and rifled through all the medical-related paperwork I did have, shoved into my handbag: bill receipts, appointment confirmations... These were all taken from me and scanned quietly, then politely returned, with the clear implication that they didn't help. I became silently frustrated and a little annoyed.

"Dr K referred me from the clinic," I insisted. "I have no letter. She just told me to call."

"Ahh! K Sensei!" they replied. No more questions asked, no more explanations needed. I was pointed in the direction of the escalator for the "breast cancer" department. Well, that came as something of a shock, to pass that sign. I don't know what I was expecting to see on it, perhaps something a little more subtly and enigmatically medical, like "mammary maladies", or "thoracic disorders". Not BREAST CANCER.

Despite having had a (modest) breakfast that morning, the journey and nervous anticipation had left me hungry. Husband bought a banana and a doughnut – I managed the banana but halfway through the doughnut felt my stomach revolting in anxiety. Husband sat with children out in the corridor waiting room* while I went into the clinical area.

A practitioner whose qualifications eluded me but who had excellent

---

* "Corridor waiting room" makes it sound very cold and impersonal. It wasn't. It was like sitting in a hotel lounge

English took me into a small room to go over my forms and ask me some questions. "I see your mum had breast cancer, and your aunt; and your grandmother died of it at… 39? I think this might be genetic."

The look she gave me was loaded with an acknowledgement that she was stating the obvious.

I replied, "Yes, I think you might be right."

"Perhaps this is something you should talk about with your doctors in the UK," she said.

(At this point I should maybe point out that I had already been part of a programme looking into the genetic causes of breast cancer. I had twice before had mammograms for screening. My doctors were well aware of the risks of me developing the disease and had done what they could to monitor the situation. But then I missed a mammogram (because of illness), and seemed to fall through the net and out of the system…)

And then I was introduced to Dr F, who would be carrying out the biopsy. She was very young, very smiley and quite giggly, apologising for her terrible English, which of course wasn't half as terrible as my non-existent Japanese. I wrote our Tokyo address on a form, but didn't know the "romaji*" translation of the apartment's name, so had to draw the katakana characters I had seen on the side of the building:

ヴィラセゾン元汎

"You have written it well," she said kindly. "I can read it. It says Villa Seasons**." What a prosaically Western name, I thought. Also a nonsensical one. "When can you come in for appointment for results?" Dr F continued.

I had a look through my diary. We were due to go to Hong Kong, then Taiwan, and on to Okinawa, the south Japanese island; then back to Tokyo

---

* Basically the use of Latin letters to write Japanese words[9]
** A quick online translation says its "Villa Saison original form" but I'm going to take Dr F's word for it

briefly before heading to South Korea.

"Lovely!" said Dr F. "But what are you doing this last month?" she pointed at my diary, where it was free of scribbling.

"Nothing. Staying in Tokyo."

"You could have your treatment here!" she said excitedly. I'm not kidding. She smiled broadly, and her eyes shone, as though she had me down as a cancer patient and booked into her treatment schedules already.

"No," I smiled and shook my head. "We can pay for all these tests but the treatment would be too expensive*. I'll have to go home."

But Dr F seemed determined to have me in a Japanese operating theatre.

"Here, we can treat you quickly, after results of tests," she said. "In Britain I think… is slower?"

Wow. Just… wow. Word of the NHS's Tory-led decrepitude has spread far and fast. But her mistrust of the British health system got my back up, a bit, especially as I remembered what my GP in Scotland had said when I visited a couple of weeks previously – that the Scottish NHS is on top of breast cancer and Edinburgh's Western General Hospital is a Centre of Excellence for the illness.

"Actually, for breast cancer the treatment can be organised very quickly," I reassured her.

She nodded, then spread out in front of me a form which explained the biopsy procedure, along with any and all complications which might occur.

It was in Japanese.

"Umm…" said Dr F, skimming through it to find any parts which I should maybe know. "Umm… one percent chance of infection, but that is very low, so…" she shrugged, continued scanning the form, then shrugged again and put the form aside.

Clearly I had nothing else to worry about. Gulp.

"Results will be ready in one week to 10 days," said Dr F.

"Will you post them to me?" I asked.

"No," she replied gravely. "For these results we need to talk to you."

I asked if I would be able to get a copy of the results to take back to the

---

* Insurance did not pay for any of the testing in Japan. We paid out of our own pockets. Strictly speaking out of husband's pocket

UK for my doctor.

"Yes," she said. "I will write them out in English and have them in PDF so you can email them. And when are you away? I will make an appointment for when you can come here."

I was delighted. These medical appointments were becoming nothing more than a scheduled part of our trip, not an inconvenience at all. We agreed on a date when I would be back from Hong Kong and Taiwan, and available to pick up the results.

And then it was time for the actual procedure. No more pleasant chatting. Take your top off and lie down on the bed. And that's when my lack of food fuelled my up-until-now suppressed anxiety, which started making itself uncomfortably known. Another nurse was called into the room, and I began to sweat, notwithstanding the soothing litany of Japanese that the nurse let flutter over me.

"Okay, so there will be some pain with anaesthetic in three, two, one..."

I clenched my teeth, but then inwardly laughed as "some pain" turned out to be the merest scratch. I waited for it to become more agonising, but it didn't. The anaesthetic was followed by three biopsy needles, which I refused to look at. Thanks to that blackout after the blood donation, I had developed something of a nervousness around needles. I can have them stuck in my arm, but I'd really rather not watch them being so.

"May be some sound of the pain in three, two..." Dr F began the countdown, and I thought, *what do you mean* sound *of the pain*? Before I could properly panic there was the boing sound of a spring, accompanied by a slight thud as it sprung.

"Oh, sound of the *spring*!" I said with relief. But with each of the three jolting thuds, I was becoming increasingly nauseated, increasingly hot and sweaty. *I'm going to faint*, I thought, *and I'm lying down*. In an effort to focus on something else and stay conscious I began clenching and unclenching my fist at my side.

I managed to stay conscious, and then it was over. The needles were removed and Dr F instructed the nurse to hold a pad on the puncture mark for five minutes. The nurse leant down hard for precisely five minutes, then Dr F covered the place with steristrips and a big pad plastered over the top.

"You will need treatment soon," she said. I looked at her.

"Do you already know? Just from the mammogram and ultrasound, and before you've got the biopsy results, that it is definitely cancer?"

Dr F nodded, with a nervous smile on her face, then left the room and returned shortly after with the English-speaking practitioner.

"I'm just here to make sure you understand everything, to ask if you have any questions," she said.

I felt a sudden pressure to ask more questions. And a concern that there were more questions to ask.

"I just wondered if she could be sure, even before the biopsy results, that it is cancer?"

The two doctors murmured rapidly to each other, and then the interpreter said, "We cannot claim to be 100% sure, but it is almost certainly cancer."

So that was that. Though, all along, I had kind of known I had cancer, maybe deep down there was a tiny glimmer of hope that the doctors could have mistaken what they'd seen on the scans – that the biopsy results would be necessary to make a final, unarguable diagnosis. Clearly not.

Perhaps it was this deep-seated realisation, the loss of control, the knowledge that the assumptions I'd had since I was 30 had finally come true, that made me feel increasingly unwell as I sat with the doctor while she wrote her notes; increasingly anxious.

Dr F looked down while she scribbled on sheets of paper and gathered various forms together, and I sat beside her becoming hotter and hotter, and fainter and fainter, knowing that both my blood sugar levels and blood pressure were uncomfortably low. I began fidgeting, made restless by the adrenalin that must have been coursing through my veins, and called husband's mobile. He didn't answer.

I felt suddenly so alone, vulnerable and embarrassed.

"I'm going to faint," I mumbled, and stuck my head between my knees.

The doctor looked up from her forms and watched me. "You are tired," she said, "you need support. Have you eaten lunch?"

"I've had a banana and half a doughnut."

Dr F let out a sort of humphing grunt, which said all that was needed about what she thought of my lunch. Her serene stillness in the face of my anxiety, her calm care, allowed me the space to draw in deep, slow breaths, until I was recovered enough to sit up and signal my willingness, my ability, to leave. Dr F walked me out to reception and said, "I will see you again soon."

Back at the apartment, I called my UK GP.

"I'm out in Japan but have been diagnosed with breast cancer," I said. "I need to be referred?" Private or NHS was the next question. I'm just going to do a bit of self-justification here, because I have never and will never stop feeling guilty for using private healthcare.

So, the question, private or NHS? Husband is self-employed, so had taken out private health insurance as a guarantee of rapid treatment, should he ever become too ill to work. Then, for reasons that escaped him, he included me in the cover, and regretted the extra expense every single year – until now.

I hummed and hawed on the phone, not wanting to say private for fear of offending the GP but accepting that, since we had been paying for private healthcare, maybe it would be foolish not to use it.

"Private!" I blurted down the phone. "No, NHS! I don't know. Will private be faster than NHS?"

"No," said my GP, quite bluntly. "We move very fast with regards to breast cancer."

"Well, I'll go private," I said.

The rest of the arrangements for my return are a blurred nonentity to me. I must have given an idea of when I would get the biopsy results, and my GP would have said how quickly I could be referred, and I decided on a date to return to Britain. But I don't recall the details; only the kindness and efficiency of my GPs and the health centre receptionist. UK referral organised, all I could do now was sit back and wait for the biopsy results.

I Aitken

The Cure

I must have had some awareness of cancer as a serious illness when I was quite small. Though I don't remember at all being affected by the death of my maternal granny – "Nanny" – she did pass away when I was three. She had ovarian cancer which metastasised throughout her body. I don't remember the impact on my family, though mum says she was ill with grief for a year afterwards. In this way, cancer became, if not part of my everyday lexicon, certainly a concept lodged firmly in the back of my wee mind.

I had a pink teddy bear. I don't think I gave her a name until I was in my teens, perhaps my twenties, when she became Annabel. As a child (I was a child, not she), she had a small, flat, brown nose made of felt. Here's what happened to her nose.

I must have been about four or five. Waking in the morning, and knowing that mum and dad were still in bed, I sat up and quietly chatted away to myself. I knew better than to get them out of bed. Being an only child until I was seven meant I was well able to play alone. I must have been watching *Tomorrow's World** a lot during this period, and been impressed by it, because I decided to pretend I was a presenter on the show. And I decided that scientists had discovered a cure for cancer (I know! What are the odds?!), which I was now demonstrating.

I peeled teddy's nose off her face and stuck it up one of my nostrils.

"And all you have to do is this!" I said proudly to the imaginary camera. "Just stick it up your nose, leave it there for a minute, and then remove it." I poked my finger up my nose and worked out the now damp

* Readers of a certain age will remember *Tomorrow's World*, the BBC's flagship science series. Maggie Philbin was my idol

piece of felt.

"It does work best if you use it in both sides," I addressed the hypothetical audience, and I poked teddy's nose up my other nostril. I posed for the camera, then stuck my finger up my nose again. But I couldn't seem to get a grip on the edge of the piece of felt – I had rammed it too far up. I poked and pushed, and eventually lost all contact with teddy's nose. I sniffed hard, but felt no obstacle. I blew, and nothing came out except snot. I sat and pondered.

I don't recall exactly what my parents' response was when I wandered into their room and woke them up, saying "Teddy's nose is stuck up my nose." I should imagine it was how I would react now if daughter woke me with those same words. They were probably nonplussed.

The result, however, was that I was taken to hospital*, where a kind doctor shone a torch up my nose and pronounced teddy's nose swallowed.

"That'll come out naturally," he said, and I understood that this meant teddy's nose would be lost forever down the toilet. "Have a sweetie for being a good girl," said the doctor, holding a big jar of Smarties in front of me. I took one Smartie, knowing that his commendation referred to my sitting nicely while he shone a torch in my nostrils, not my act of shoving a piece of felt up my nose and pretending it was a cure for cancer.

* Neither mum nor dad drove, so the trip would have been made by taxi or in a neighbour's car – nobody can remember

Chapter Three

The next nearly three weeks were a round of sensory overload, with sights, sounds and experiences that were all-enveloping and a very successful distraction from the issue of the potential biopsy results. Just our arrival on Hong Kong Island was enough to wipe all other thoughts from my mind. Not only was it so different from the UK, it was entirely different from Japan, a situation which inexplicably surprised me. It was louder, brasher, ruder, dirtier. More real. I was shocked when we stood waiting for a train into the city from the airport, and an old man turned to a lad behind him and started yelling. We hadn't heard yelling at all in Tokyo. That realisation was unexpected.

The train ride took us through a landscape that was oddly tropical and also industrial: mountains with fronds of smoggy clouds as head dresses, the slopes' sides textured and coloured by trees; the tamed seas, reclaimed and pushed back; and masses of high rises, building sites, cranes and construction. It was a fascinatingly unusual terrain, but also faintly depressing – to see a sort of sumptuous vista defaced by grey concrete and metal.

Hong Kong was brazen. Busy. Noisy. And crawling with high-performance cars: Porsches, Teslas and Lamborghinis roared from red lights only to be halted 10m on by another red light. Their power was comically pointless.

The proximity of poverty to wealth was dizzying – the flats above the high-end, luxury Longines store were a slab of peeling paint, cakes of dirt, and trees growing from the gutters…

I found the people much more rude. More rude than the Japanese, that is, and perhaps even ruder than the Brits (mate, London shopkeepers/ bartenders/bankers really aren't that friendly). One diner scowled at the waitress in a restaurant; we ourselves were scowled at by a waiter in another restaurant; the concierge at the first hotel we stayed in was indifferent to the point of insulting, and didn't once look us in the face as he took our credit card. I mean, you know, I don't expect grovelling gratitude but I do expect acknowledgement of our humanity.

Anyway, my distaste aside, we were entertained by visits to Victoria Peak via the Peak Tram; unidentifiable and inexplicable seafood alive and thrashing in boxes at the harbour; the daily, usually unsuccessful hunt for good, honest breakfast tea; silken swirls of Indonesian workers gathered in Victoria Square on their Sunday off; a community art project at a former abattoir in Kowloon; by street stalls which offended my sensitive, Western, pescatarian nose with boxes of chicken and pigs' heads; and by a 3am exodus from our unwelcoming hotel to another one round the corner, shepherding our pyjama-clad children through the finally silent streets of the city.

From Hong Kong we flew to Taipei, where husband was attending a conference for a couple of days. I learned a lot about the history of Taiwan[*] in the short time we were there, inspired by a conversation with a taxi driver, who compared Scotland's occasional break for independence with the Taiwan/China relationship (though only after he finally remembered where Scotland is).

"Ah yes, Scotland at the top of UK," he said. "It is different from rest of UK. Like Taiwan and China – we are Taiwanese, not Chinese."

And it really did feel like a totally different nation; we were back to being treated politely, by kind, calm, helpful, friendly folk, rather than the shouty ones of Hong Kong.

In Taipei, too, we encountered a plethora of unidentifiable food stuffs, which even the most adventurous among us were loath to try, despite the fact that the queues for the street stalls selling said foodstuffs were up to 100m long. Such queues might have been an indication of the quality of the delicacies on offer, but we weren't going to risk it.

Our stay in Taipei was too short to truly experience all that Taiwan had

---

[*] It used to belong to China, then Japan, and now China thinks Taiwan belongs to it again, but Taiwan thinks it's in charge of China. It's all very complicated and extremely interesting

to offer; but the thought of what news there was for me back in Tokyo was held at bay by visits to the Night Market, the Museum of Miniatures, and Taipei 101, the world's fifth tallest building, an excursion which was almost pointless thanks to the cloudiness of the day, but fortunately saw some break in the cloud cover so we could glimpse snatches of the city hundreds of feet below.

From Taipei we flew to Okinawa, a Japanese island and prefecture 954 miles south-west of Tokyo. Okinawa is a paradise; a paradise pockmarked by 32 US army bases. We had little to do with those, though – we ignored the barbed wire fencing and grey block buildings and immersed ourselves in a blindingly teal ocean, snorkelling in the placid shallows of the East China Sea. It was my first time snorkelling, and my fear of the ocean was put to rest by the serenity, and the audacious fishes, which delighted me with their vibrant hues as they darted at the food held in my outstretched hands.

It was a magical place. Is a magical place. The dichotomy of its natural beauty and the manmade evidence of war and aggression was occasionally jarring, but the island and its inhabitants seemed unperturbed by the barbed wire and guns. "Do the Okinawans like the Americans being here?" we asked our taxi driver. "Half half," he said. "We don't need them." We flew back to Tokyo vowing to return to Okinawa and explore more of its untouched allure.

One night's sleep in Tokyo, then back to St Luke's Hospital for the biopsy results. The previous three weeks of travel had been so successfully distracting, I entered the room with the consultant and interpreter smilingly lighthearted.

No sooner had husband and I sat down than Dr F said that yes, the biopsy results confirmed I had breast cancer. "Do you have any questions?" she asked.

Naturally, in a situation like that there must be hundreds of questions. But how was I supposed to know what they were? Fortunately, my silence did not bring the meeting to an end. As half an hour passed, more thoughts occurred to me, and Dr F and the interpreter answered each question kindly and attentively.

Yes, Dr F would provide the results via email and PDF printout for my

UK doctor; yes, this was a primary cancer but I would need further tests to ascertain whether it had metastasised elsewhere in my body; the scans had shown inflammation of my lymph glands, so those should be tested further in the UK; the lump was 2.25cm.

This last fact was the one that shocked me most, since I have very small boobs and I couldn't understand why a lump 2.25cm large wouldn't have stuck out like a sore thumb. Instead it had clawed in the surrounding tissue, sucking the breast mass into the black hole of the tumour, causing the dimple that grew under my stupidly apathetic eye.

Dr F referred again to the likelihood of genetic predisposition, and pointed out that, were I having treatment in Japan, they would test for mutations of the BRCA genes*, which result would determine what treatment I should receive. I left the hospital with a wad of notes and a CD of scan images, both of which, perhaps oddly, gave me a sense of being fully armed and prepared for whatever fight there was ahead of me.

But then I had to make the call I sincerely didn't want to. I phoned my mum.

"Hi mum, I have breast cancer," I said, as calmly as I could.

"Hello angel, how are you?! What was that?"

"I've got breast cancer!" I prepared myself for the intake of breath and the hopeless tears, and will never forget how surprised, delighted and proud I felt when she replied,

"Okay, calm down…" (I wasn't surprised, delighted and proud of that, 'cos I fecking hate being told to calm down and, besides which, I wasn't being not calm at that moment, but anyway) "… and don't worry. We can do this – you can do this – the doctors are brilliant and the treatment works. It will all be fine." That was exactly what I needed to hear at that moment, 5735 miles away from my mum and terrified that breaking my news to her over the phone would lead to her distress and my sense of guilt.

"We arrive home the day after tomorrow," I said, "and I have an

---

* The BRCA1 and BRCA2 genes are tumour suppressors. Certain (but not all) mutations of these genes can lead to breast and/or ovarian cancer. Such mutations are inherited from either parent. If the mutation is detected, the patient could be given the option for a mastectomy, to reduce the risk of breast cancer. This does not mean, however, that they wouldn't potentially pass the gene to any children[10]

appointment with a consultant the day after that. So the wheels are all turning."

Phonecall over. Shoulders back. Head up. Deep breath. And off to pack our bags for the flight home the next day.

I Aitken

The "Epidemic"

Of course, mum's incredible stoicism was not just a facet of her character. In fact, stoicism is not usually one of the first words that come to mind when describing her. But, on this occasion, she had good reason to allay her fears and remain calm – she had already been through it. In fact, in the previous six or so years, she had been through a lot.

In 2010, I was pregnant with daughter. Heavily pregnant. Heavily pregnant, grumpy, uncomfortable and touchy. I was with husband, visiting his sister and family at her house in the city, when I got a phonecall from mum.

She said she'd been diagnosed with breast cancer.

I don't remember much of that call, aside from the tone of mum's voice. She was scared – of her illness? Of telling me? – and also having to manage my response as well as her own emotions. It must have been one of the hardest calls she's ever made. If I had had even the slightest hint of compassion, I would have put myself in her shoes and been slightly more sympathetic in my response. She would have been frightened about her diagnosis, and what treatment was to come, and nervous about telling me, especially since I was about to have a baby. She would have made the fairly safe assumption that I would overreact, and god knows she wouldn't have wanted to deal with excess emotion. She must have taken such a deep breath before making that call, had shaking fingers while dialling the number. She would not have wanted me to travel so far to be with her but knew I would feel guilty about not doing so. When I think about it now, I finally understand how much pressure she was under.

And, of course, I didn't think about it then. I didn't put myself in her shoes at all. I was inexplicably and selfishly angry. Angry at her? Why? I think it was the timing that annoyed me, not that mum could do anything about that, of course. For a start I took the call when I wasn't at home, which would have been preferable. I would have felt more at leisure to cry or rant.

And then there was the fact that she was 400 miles away, so I was utterly impotent.

And, to top it all off, I was heavily pregnant, and awash with all the hormones and emotions being in such a state entails. I couldn't rail at mum, because it wasn't her fault, and I couldn't rail at the gods, because I'm an atheist… Who or what could I blame?

In the end – and I am deeply ashamed of this – I did nothing to comfort my mum. While she was going through two surgeries and radiotherapy, I was having my baby and being utterly wrapped up in all the turmoil that engendered. I didn't travel home to see her, even for a long weekend. I purposefully stayed out of it, I consciously made the decision that I couldn't emotionally handle my mum being ill while I was struggling with sleepless nights and nappy changes.

Not once did I see her during her months of illness and treatment.

And at the time I let that fact slide by without a thought or pang of conscience, but now that I've been through it myself, I can't believe my heartlessness, am ashamed of being so thoughtless and self-obsessed.

And, of course, mum's cancer was just the start of an avalanche of ill health among her nearest and dearest. Honestly, how she hasn't just thrown in the towel and sacked the lot of us, I've no idea.

Just a couple of months after she had finished her treatment for DCIS*, and only a few months after the birth of daughter, I was walking with friends on the beach, our toddler children scrambling over the rocks. Another awkward time and place to receive a truly horrible phonecall from mum, who, when I answered my mobile, said brother had a brain tumour. I didn't handle this very well. My baby was still young enough to make sleeping erratic and therefore my emotional state quite… not hysterical, I hate that word, but I certainly wasn't very calm.

---

* Ductal carcinoma in situ – cancer cells completely contained in the breast lobules and ducts[11]

For a couple of days I was floating on a tide of uncertainty, again feeling that distance from my family… but not enough to make the 400-mile journey to support them.

As it turns out, brother didn't have a brain tumour. It was slightly more complex than that.

He had, for a while, been struck with debilitating migraines. He had never had a migraine in all his life until this period in his 30th year, when they suddenly appeared. They were especially bad after his Sunday local league football matches, so there was some assumption among us that he was just dehydrated. But they got so bad he went to see his GP. I think he saw his GP several times during this period, obviously with some sort of niggling sensation that it couldn't just be a migraine. But that's exactly what they were, said his GP, who sent brother home to take paracetamol and stop wasting his time.

Eventually brother decided to make use of his employer's private health insurance and had a consultation with a neurology specialist, who took one deep look with a torch into brother's eyes and told him he would have to be admitted for emergency surgery the very next day.

What brother had been suffering was not migraines but hydrocephalus[12]. His head was full of cerebrospinal fluid. (I mean, I could have told him this. Sometimes he responds with all the emotional sensitivity of a bowlful of soup.)

Here's how it happened: our bodies produce cerebrospinal fluid all day, every day – it protects the brain, and feeds it nutrients. To aid the circulation of fresh fluid, the skull contains valves, or ducts, which drain the old fluid away. (This is a v simple description which will no doubt have the neurologists among you howling with contempt[13]) Unfortunately, brother's valve had been blocked by a benign cyst, and so the plughole, as it were, was blocked and excess fluid failing to drain away. I can picture his head filling up like a lethal bath. If it had been left only a matter of days more, the pressure on his brain would have become so great he would… well, I can't really say it.

Good news: the cyst was benign. Bad news: it was in too sensitive a position to be removed by surgery, without risking brain damage in the process. So brother's life-saving brain surgery involved draining the fluid from his head, then inserting a shunt[14] – a narrow pipe which extends from within his skull, under his skin down through his neck and shoulder, into his stomach, and which takes over the job of draining the liquid. He will have this shunt in place for the rest of his life. A shunt that will always be at risk of being past its sell-by date and introducing infection. It is a state that necessarily comes with permanent worry.

But it doesn't stop there! Of course it doesn't!

A couple years of recovery from that shitshow of a year and then it was dad's turn. He had an odd lump on his forearm, which was eventually diagnosed as merkel cell carcinoma (MCC)[15], a rare and aggressive skin cancer. Further inspection revealed an incredible depth to the cancer; his specialist (a consultant plastic surgeon I'm calling Mr T) was concerned that it was actually a secondary cancer – his understanding of MCC was that it began as a tumour on the vital organs. This, of course, was devastating. Primary cancer is bad enough but secondary, or metastatic, cancer is v bad news, often with much worse prognoses.

Dad was sent for an MRI to scan his internal bits. He was immediately handed the results, which he took with him back to the consultant… who was away on holiday for three weeks. So, unable to interpret the MRI results, dad had to wait three weeks to find out what the problem was and if it was curable.

Mr T having returned from his lengthy fiesta, he took a look at the scan results and was able to deliver some surprisingly good news. Even he was surprised. There were no other tumours. This deeply embedded lump in dad's arm was the primary cancer. Then it was just a case of removing it. Ha! Easy peasy…

But you should see the scar. It's massive. And the surgery involved the most fascinating process, called the propeller flap[16] – which was developed by Mr T himself, so dad was in safe surgical hands.

Said treatment consisted of the cancer being cut out of dad's arm; then an incision made around a large square of skin just above the wound, and this skin being lifted and twisted round to cover the now cancer-free hole. It's a process that usually engenders better results for grafting, since it's using the patient's own skin and maintaining blood supply, as the donor site remains attached in a small corner. Here's the best bit, though – to encourage blood flow through the newly placed skin, leeches were placed on it. Seriously. There is no better medical process than this archaic one. dad said it was a bit weird when the leech was taken off him and placed in a pot and he could see his blood running down the inside of said pot. And once a nurse accidentally dropped a leech in his bed and there was a scuffle to avoid it latching onto his buttocks. But isn't that awesome? This is what I love about science and medicine. If it ain't broke, don't fix it*.

Suffice it to say, despite some pretty scary assumptions at the beginning of dad's diagnosis, he was soon fully mended, but now bears a substantial and rather ugly scar, advertising the necessity for suntan lotion**...

But that wasn't all! Of course not! There's still a bit to go in this particular chapter! Take a deep breath and read on...

The very next year, brother – that very same brother who had already had to undergo massive surgery to drain a headful of fluid – noticed blood in his semen. Incredibly sensibly, he visited the GP, who referred him for an ultrasound. This scan revealed an area of "irregularity" in one of the testes, but the urologist was not convinced it was cancerous, so brother was sent off with the advice to return in six months for further tests. Six months later, the ultrasound scan revealed that the "irregularity" had grown – he was diagnosed with testicular cancer. He was 32.

Fortunately the tumour was a small one – brother was never aware of there having been a lump – so his testicle was removed and the cancer contained with no need for further treatment such as chemo or radiotherapy. And as it turns out, his urologist was of the opinion that the bloody semen was entirely unrelated and unimportant, so it was really pure chance that brother's cancer was diagnosed. Lads – if there's ever anything unusual or irregular about your balls and all that they produce, flipping see your GP.

Brother is now slightly lop-sided but has two beautiful children, is still here with us, and I will have to put up with his sarcasm and foul-mouthed insults until the end of my days.

The above is a fairly flippant way of explaining the immensity that is

---

* Even more exciting, dad's surgery took place in The McIndoe Centre – Archibald McIndoe was a brilliant doctor whose revolutionary grafting techniques were used during World War II to mend burns suffered by fighter pilots[17]

** Most MCCs are caused by sun exposure

testicular cancer. I can't say that brother's illness is that easily and tidily packaged. As it were. I was told very little about what was happening at the time, and I've never yet had a profound conversation with him on the matter – I'm not sure he'd want to talk about it; and I'm also not sure that it would be fair to ascribe thoughts or feelings to him. To assume what he went through and what he's going through now. But just like I didn't put myself in mum's shoes until it was too late, I can now make a fair stab at understanding how brother has been affected by his ill health. Cancer leaves emotional scarring that is far deeper and uglier than the physical stuff. It takes a long time to recover from the trauma of the diagnosis, the worries about the prognosis, the hideousness of the treatment, the potential impacts – mental, financial, etc – on a young family… It's a lot to live with.

(Interestingly, having communicated via email with brother about this period in his life, he avers that the cancer was as nothing compared with the psychological trauma of the hydrocephalus. "Because there was just the surgery and I didn't feel sick, and I never had to have chemo or radio, I've never really felt that affected by the testicular thing," he says. "It's very much the hydrocephalus illness and resulting treatment that stayed with me, mentally." That was so much more traumatic, so much more a delicate procedure, with a lifelong impact.)

And then there were four peaceful years, years my family spent recovering from the emotional impact of the sum total of ill health, and being grateful for their good fortune in surviving. And then I had to make the phonecall from Tokyo to mum. And after everything she had been through for the previous seven years, she had the knowledge, the confidence, the resilience and courage to to be my own strength and positivity.

But by the end of my treatment, when I was also cured, she said, "I'm not calling myself lucky any more. I don't think we've been lucky at all." She had a point.

Chapter Four

The long plane journey back to the UK was a contemplative one. I had no fear of what was to come; what I did have was a degree of sorrow that we were leaving Japan so soon. I felt as though I had cheated the rest of my family out of the trip they had expected and deserved. I sat crying my way through several movies – "*La La Land* is so sad! Why did nobody tell me how sad *La La Land* is!" I sobbed – blotting my ability to think about what we were leaving or what I would be returning to.

The family staying in our house while we were away would not be able to leave for another couple of days, so we booked a hotel between the airport and my consultant's clinic for a couple of nights. Mother-in-law came to meet us at the hotel to take the children, and husband began making calls to the health insurance company. I couldn't deal with such admin. I couldn't answer questions, or accept responsibility for the bureaucracy involved. My mind, those couple of days, was stodgy and unfathomable; unable to think clearly or rationally, I was incapable of talking calmly to the woman on the end of the phone at the insurance company. My voice raised, and I became petulant, even as her own tone remained low and calm.

This was as much to do with the 15-hour journey and 11-hour time difference as it was to do with preparing for what was to come.

The evening after our touchdown in Edinburgh, husband and I went for our first consultation with the man who was to become my surgeon, Mr A. I don't think I took this meeting entirely seriously. Actually, looking back, I think I was perhaps slightly hysterical. I was smiley, and giggly, and whispered cheesy jokes into husband's ear as he checked work emails on his phone:

"Worst pub I've ever been to was called The Fiddle. It really was a vile inn," snigger, snigger. "A horse limps into a bar with a bandage round his head. He orders a glass of Champagne, a vintage brandy and two pints of Guinness. He downs the lot and says to the barman: 'I shouldn't really be drinking this with what I've got.' 'Why?' asks the barman. 'What have you got?' 'About two quid and a carrot.'" Chortle chortle*.

I thought I was being lighthearted and breezy but in all likelihood I was shitscared and in denial.

I had emailed Mr A the PDF of all my scan and biopsy results from the wonderful Tokyo doctors, so naturally I assumed that as soon as I walked in he would be *au fait* with my case and doling out solutions. Not quite. We sat down, and he turned to his computer and began scrolling through emails, scans and messages, humming and nodding. A couple of times he snickered at the English translation, which I thought a tad rude. Even I could understand the reports, and I'm not a medic.

"We'll have to get our own scans done because sometimes these ones… well…" he said. "I had a patient who was diagnosed somewhere in Africa and the scans were just incomprehensible." Because of course Japan is in Africa.

Now my back was up for two reasons: 1) he had taken the piss out of the translation, when I was willing to bet the only Japanese words he knew were sushi and karate; and 2) he was suggesting that I go through the entire scan process all over again.

But I said nothing. Nothing assertive, anyway. What I wanted to say was, I've been through enough already. I've been poked, prodded and pricked. I know what I've got, you know what I've got, don't put me through all that yet again.

What I actually did was make my way to the x-ray department for an ultrasound scan. My awkwardness at Dr C being a man was alleviated by our conversation about his pink shirt; I don't know if his references to his teenaged daughters were intended to put me at ease, but they actually did. (It seems crazy that one should expect a man to respect a woman if he has a wife and daughters – why wouldn't he respect a woman because she's human?) He scanned my right breast and armpit – correct medical name, "axilla" – but didn't spend as long as the Japanese radiologist had done, going over and over the same spot. He did, however, zoom in, zoom out and click various points on the screen. So there it was. The lump.

He peered at the image of my right axilla lymph nodes, which had been reported as inflamed, and said, "Those look fine. They are within the range of what I'd expect. We won't need to do a biopsy there." I felt a huge surge of relief, remembering with some trepidation the anxiety that had accompanied the biopsy in Tokyo.

Then an ultrasound of my left breast, within which the Japanese scans had detected some sort of mass ("There is shadows in your left breast but that is nothing," Dr K had said). This had been diagnosed by the Tokyo doctors as an intraductal papilloma[18], a small benign tumour that forms in the milk ducts. But Dr C was not certain what this mass was, and since it is NICE[19] policy to remove intraductal papillomas[20], even though they don't necessarily lead to cancer, he would need to take a biopsy of this area. Well, bollocks. First, though, a tiny piece of titanium would be injected into the site as a marker. I expected to feel the agonising sensation of a lump of metal being forcibly inserted into my breast, but instead experienced the merest scratch, which set my mind at rest for the biopsy, which came next.

The biopsy needle was pushed into my breast.

"Is that okay?" asked Dr C. "It's not sore?"

"I can't feel a thing," I said. "Much like my first sexual encounter." I'm sorry, I just couldn't help it. You'd have thought that, being in this vulnerable, semi-dressed position I would have wandered as far away from the subject of sex as possible, but it turns out that no, my way of dealing with this situation was to make the doctor feel even more embarrassed and awkward than I did.

Dr C's shoulders began shaking with laughter, while he fought to steady the needle in my breast. "I'm not sure that's appropriate," he said.

I stood up, and Dr C explained what the scans meant and what might happen next. "It might be beneficial to have an MRI because that can see better through breast tissue, and you have quite dense breast tissue…" Dr C's eyes veered away from me to the corner of the room.

"Shall I put my clothes back on?" I asked.

"Yes, yes please," he said. No naked humans here, please. Only cases.

Fully clothed, I returned to Mr A's room and explained that Dr C hadn't been worried about the lymph nodes. "Oh," I said, "but is he a Doctor or a Mister?" It's a crucial difference in the medical world, apparently.

"He's just a Doctor," said Mr A dismissively. And Dr C's very existence, let alone status, was swept aside. "We'll have the results of your papilloma biopsy in a few days. There's a tiny, tiny chance it could be a small cancer but it'll be removed anyway, when we perform the operation on your right breast."

I didn't know what to make of Mr A. He was very public school, younger than I would have expected, with a brisk manner that rather made me feel as though I was on a conveyor belt. He did, in fact, refer to the many, many operations he had performed on women in my situation, blasé about their importance and outcomes.

When he called my cancer "bog standard", though, I bridled.

"There is nothing bog standard about this body," I said tartly. I don't have anything like an amazing body but I think it's a bit belittling for a doctor to call even the cancerous bit of a patient bog standard. He back-pedalled satisfyingly.

One question I had was how long he thought the cancer had been in my breast. The Japanese doctors had suggested it had been present for up to 10 years.

"No, no, no," he spluttered. "A year, at most." That is quite a large discrepancy, and one I have never been able to solve.

Mr A went on to explain the process from here on, referring to the cancer as unaggressive, rather than bog standard. Its size would enable a simple lumpectomy, during which the cancer would be removed, and the hole it left being filled with fat removed from my leg…

"Wait, what?" I asked. I don't have an amazing body but my best and most favourite part is my legs. (*Are* my legs?) They are all muscle, and hardly any fat. The thought of them being dragged into this process was alarming. "Um, no. Not the leg. You don't touch these legs. Can you get some fat from my belly? There's plenty there."

"We do usually use the legs, but yes, we can use fat from your belly, if you like," said Mr A. Ding ding! That was me, taking control. I smiled serenely.

Mr A continued. "I'll be talking to your oncologist next week…" I had an oncologist? *Who? And what's an oncologist?* "…and will discuss with them whether we should treat you with chemotherapy first, to shrink the tumour. That would make surgery easier. The chemo would be a four-month process, before surgery. If your oncologist decides you don't need chemo beforehand, when we remove your lump we'll take out some lymph nodes as well, to test them and see whether you need chemo afterwards."

I remember thinking that chemo just wouldn't come into it. That word – chemotherapy – was haunting, a damning term that evoked visions of nausea and baldness. I didn't believe I would have to go through that.

We had been joined by DE, a clinic nurse associated with Macmillan, a lovely, warm presence in the room, who laughed at my dry humour. She suggested I organise having a BRCA test[21], to see if I carried the mutated gene that causes breast cancer. Since I was convinced my cancer was hereditary, I thought this was a good idea, but Mr A said confidently, "I don't think you have it."

"But if I did have it, would it have an impact on my treatment?" I asked.

"Yes. It would make risk reduction surgery – a mastectomy – a factor."

And just as I had ruled out the possibility of having chemotherapy, I immediately ruled in the probability that I would have to have both breasts removed. But this damning self-prognosis wasn't too unsettling. Despite Mr A's occasionally dismissive tone, he clearly knew what he was talking about, and it is heartening to put one's life in the hands of an experienced professional. The probable treatments were sketched so clearly, I felt as though the process to get rid of the cancer had practically begun. I left his office feeling more relaxed than when we went in.

When we returned home, the tsunami of support from friends began building up speed and strength. They had been alerted to my diagnosis by the blog I wrote during our trip to Japan, and were ready and waiting with meals and hugs. What can we do, they asked. Do you need food? Childcare? There were two boxes of dinners already in our freezer upon our return. Bunches of flowers were lined up on the doorstep, by people too sensitive and sympathetic to bother us by ringing the doorbell. Our vases having been packed in the attic before our trip abroad, containers for the flowers were also donated. Such colours arrayed on the kitchen table – the confectionery purple of an exploding lily, tiger-speckled lemon yellow of alstromeria, the blushing pink red of some upright tulips – were physical signs of the love for our family, and succeeded in reminding me I was not alone.

My erudite brother sent me an email demanding I keep him up-to-date with the treatment, since, having had cancer himself, he was now morbidly fascinated with the illness and its treatment. (I made that last bit up.) "What a silly word 'lumpectomy' is," he wrote. "'I'm afraid it's bad news. You've got a bad case of lump.'" He followed up this email with one that explained the etymology of that awful word.

"I am reading a book called *The Emperor Of All Maladies*[22] which is essentially a biography of cancer. I found out from this book that the term 'lumpectomy' was initially coined as a pejorative term by US cancer researchers.

"Apparently, the initial orthodoxy when it came to surgical interventions for breast cancer was to perform 'radical mastectomies' which were pretty brutal. They felt that the best course of action was to remove as much tissue as possible (breast, lymph glands, chest muscles, connective tissues, sometimes even ribs!).

"Then a clever British surgeon started doing smaller-scale surgery that focused more directly on the tumour alone. The US scientists dismissed this with the joking term 'lumpectomy' as if it was somehow unscientific."

So there you go. A pejorative term. An insult. Now commonly used in surgery. Well, I wasn't having any of that.

Less than a week after my first appointment with Mr A, I was back in the clinic's waiting room with husband, again buzzing with adrenalin and fear, which I converted into mild hysteria and dirty jokes.

"I hate getting old," I whispered into husband's ear, as he scanned his phone's screen. "I was at a lap-dancing club last night and as I tucked a tenner into her underwear she whispered, 'Come upstairs with me and I'll give you super sex.' 'Thanks,' I said. 'I'll have the soup.'"

I snorted with laughter while husband looked up to check no-one else had heard.

My humorous mood was stifled somewhat when we sat down in Mr A's room.

"I've looked again at the pictures and the lump is much bigger than I thought," he said. "Closer to four or five centimetres. That would mean a mastectomy."

"Fuck," I said.

"Fuck," Mr A agreed.

"Well, that makes all the questions I had about the lumpectomy kind of redundant," I said. "Talking of which, did you know that lumpectomy is a pejorative term?" And I regaled him with a summary of what my brother had told me. "So I don't want to call it a lumpectomy any more. What is the medical term?"

A small, enigmatic smile played around the edges of Mr A's mouth. "A wide local excision," he said, and I made a point of writing this down in my notepad. Since there is a medical term for the procedure, why wasn't it used?

But my obsession with the semantics could not disguise a deep-seated fear that I would now indeed be having a mastectomy. The 15-minute conversation that followed Mr A's pronouncement passed me by – I have no recollection and no notes of what was said. I thought that I had already convinced myself that I would be having a mastectomy, but I was still taken aback. To have the doctor's opinion underpin my own made it more real – and also more shocking, since at our previous appointment he had assured me I would only be undergoing a lumpectomy. Wide local excision.

And what was all this about the lump being four or five centimetres? What had happened to the 2.25cm that the Japanese doctors had diagnosed? Had it honestly grown that much in a couple of weeks? Images of a Day of the Triffids-type malignant tumour came to mind, an aggressive organism that doubled in size each week, eating me from the inside out.

"We'll need another mammogram, just to make sure," said Mr A, looking at his computer screen.

At this point I was rather overwhelmed by disgust for this… thing inside me.

"If I'm having a mastectomy, I want both of them off," I said bluntly. Apparently this is not an unusual response. Well, when you're told that what you thought was a manageable lump in your breast is now markedly bigger, you really don't want to entertain the possibility of another one popping up in the other breast. If the breast is where they make themselves at home, remove both of them.

Mr A nodded, with something approaching understanding. "Well, it's a possibility. Some people might like to spend some time thinking about it."

"I don't need to think," I said. "I make my decisions quickly."

"She does," said husband.

"You're young," said Mr A. "A mastectomy is a serious undertaking, it does alter your physical sensations, and it does need upkeep." He wasn't saying I couldn't have one, but he was, responsibly, outlining the drawbacks in an attempt to slow down my thunderous train of thought.

Mr A consulted the private clinic and NHS hospital[*] schedules on his computer to find out when a double mastectomy could be performed – not for a few more weeks, he said, which might necessitate having chemo first, to halt the cancer's progress. Which would be a shame, he continued, since the oncologist he'd talked to had suggested I wouldn't need chemo until after the op, if at all.

(But if I didn't need chemo till after the op, surely that would have meant the tumour was only 2.25cm after all? A 4cm lump would definitely have needed shrinking before surgery. Hmm. I didn't think of this at the time.)

There was too much talking. Too many figures. Too many decisions that were apparently all mine to make.

"The mammogram," I said. The mammogram would decide for us all.

This was a less uncomfortable affair than the one I had undergone in Tokyo. Less bashing about, and poking into position – but still a degree of pinching that felt as though, in addition to my breast, my entire upper arm and armpit were being aggressively sandwiched between two metal plates.

There was a 20-minute wait afterwards, while the results were sent to Mr A and he quickly had a consultation with another patient. My frantic sense of jocularity was apparently impervious to all threats of having body parts removed, since I continued "entertaining" husband with jokes gleaned from Popbitch.

"What's green and doesn't weigh very much? Light green. What's made of brass and sounds like Tom Jones? Trombones." Husband smiled wanly, while checking his emails.

When we returned to Mr A's room, "No," he said, "it is less than three centimetres, you'll only need a lumpectomy. Sorry, a wide local excision."

---

[*] Mr A works in both

A rainbow of emotions swept over me. One hour before I had been told that I would probably have to lose whole body parts – now I would be undergoing the merest little surgical procedure. The immediate relief was swept aside by anger, confusion, and then resignation.

Having summoned my thoughts, I said, "So I just have the… wide local excision," (I had to consult with my notes to remember this), "and the papilloma in my left breast removed at the same time?"

"No," said Mr A. "There is no papilloma. The biopsy showed that the small mass there is just a fibroadenoma." I had to look this up afterwards – it's a harmless, benign lump[23].

"What about the titanium?" I asked. Nobody had said anything about that tiny marker inserted in my breast. "Does that stay there?"

"Yes," said Mr A, "it's harmless. It's not even really classed as a metal." Whaaaat?

The brain is a strange thing. Also a very clever thing. Faced with the overwhelming rainbow of emotions, it turned its back and focused on the least important aspect of the conversation. I became fascinated by this piece of metal-not-classed-as-metal that was now permanently lodged in my body.

"Will it set off airport scanners?" I asked.

"No. I have a metal bolt in my shoulder, and that never sets it off."
I pondered on the metal-not-classed-as-metal bolt in his shoulder, and concluded that he must be a rugby player. Of course he was.

"Could I give you one more examination?" asked Mr A. I eyed him cautiously. Why? What else would he hope to discover?

"Just so we know what we're dealing with," added Mr A.

"A boob," I said bluntly. Surely that much was obvious. Mr A sighed. I think by this point he had the measure of me, and realised I might be something of an awkward customer.

Having examined me once more, he explained that since I would not be having a mastectomy after all, and just a wide local excision, this could be performed the following week.

"So we'll just take out the cancer, along with some lymph nodes to check those, then fill the hole with fat from your leg…"

"Uh uh uh! Not the leg. You don't touch these legs."

"… With fat from your belly," Mr A corrected himself, "and after five weeks you'll undergo radiotherapy."

But of course there would also be the BRCA gene test, and then the testing of the lump and lymph nodes, which would reveal more about the source and development of the cancer, and whether I would then need chemo and/or a mastectomy.

"And because your cancer is oestrogen receptive, you will take tamoxifen daily for five years after treatment has finished," Mr A concluded. By this time my brain was saturated with information. There were too many alternate avenues we might have to go down, too many ifs and buts. Not to mention the sudden mastectomy which had loomed over me, followed by the equally sudden less drastic, easily packaged treatment solution.

Confused and exhausted, I nevertheless left the clinic high on the sensation that, whatever the method, I would be cured.

The Fall

Confidence in my longevity was perhaps influenced by the fact I had already cheated death a couple of times before. Well, death might be stretching it in the case of getting my teeth knocked out by a swing when I was a toddler, but I did, somewhat miraculously, survive another, quite impressive, accident.

When I was pregnant with son, I had recurring minor pregnancy-related health niggles, one of which was a persistent urinary tract infection. On one occasion, this became so bad I was physically sick – I phoned the health centre, desperate for a doctor to come out to where I was staying, in temporary accommodation out in the middle of nowhere.

The receptionist was adamant the GP couldn't do that.

"You can see the duty doctor in the cottage hospital," she said. I, reluctantly, contacted mother-in-law, and cadged a lift into town.

Fortuitously, as I sat on the bed in the hospital, I threw up again. The doctor prodded at my kidneys and suggested I go to the city Infirmary for scans.

"Serious UTIs can cause contractions, which can lead to premature labour," he said cautiously. An ambulance was called.

"I have a question," I said. "I fractured my pelvis in three places about nine years ago – will that have an impact on my pregnancy? Will the bump put a strain on the bones? Will I be able to have a normal labour?"

"I should think so," said the doctor, I hoped answering the third question. "How did you do that?"

"I fell off a roof," I said sheepishly.

"As a child?"

"No. I was 23. And drunk."

The doctor and mother-in-law exchanged glances.

"Old enough to know better," said mother-in-law (the first and only time I have ever known her judge me). I, lying on my back, with my bump exposed like a small fleshy hillock removing any sense of self-esteem, felt humiliated.

And the full tale of the fall isn't any less shameful. It was like this.

I did an NVQ in journalism, a three-and-a-half month course at a small training centre in Mitcham, Surrey. Yes, Mitcham. You know, the epicentre of news and media revelations. Those three-and-a-half months were a hedonist blast, involving new friends, nights out and journalistic pretensions. The boyfriend I somehow attracted on this course had a pal who had a mum who had a flat in Pimlico, London. We had already made use of this flat for party reasons; at this point I need to explain the structure of the flat.

It was one of those gorgeous Georgian terraced buildings that litter Pimlico; four storeys (40 feet) high. The pal's mum's flat was on the very top floor, with no immediate access to the flat roof. I say immediate access – we discovered that you could climb out the sitting room windows, which were shielded at the front by a low wall, and scramble up onto the roof. Once there you could drink gin and dance. Then you could drop down through the skylight onto an armchair placed strategically under it near the kitchen.

A rudimentary sketch* of the building can be found at *plate i*.

Please note at the base of the building the iron railings, positioned some three or four feet from the front of the wall.

So. We had climbed onto the roof once or twice before this night. I was fearless because I was young, so obviously immortal. On this occasion, I had to borrow a pair of jeans from boyfriend's pal, as I was wearing an impractical short skirt. I was sensible like that. There were five of us, if I recall. Which I don't. I mean, I think there were five of us – boyfriend, three of his mates and me. But I could be wrong, since my memory is understandably hazy and unreliable.

We climbed onto the roof and I proceeded to get up close and personal

---

* Compiled using InDesign, an application which allows those with skill to create amazing diagrams and images. I have little skill

with a bottle of Bombay Sapphire gin.

(I just drifted off then, as I recalled the sense of freedom and joy at that time. The feeling of anarchy; the sophistication of the blue glass gin bottle; the glory of being young and happy; the intoxication of, not just the alcohol, but the idea that that summer was the start of the rest of my life. I was beginning the career in journalism I had dreamed of for years. Nothing could stop me.)

I don't need to explain what happens when one gets drunk. The loss of inhibitions, sense and perspective. So I started doing handstands on the roof. Look, I was young and flexible. I had the energy in those days. The handstands moved on to a cartwheel or two. It was a big enough roof.

Then I said, "I'm going to do an Arab spring*."

I launched myself into the run-up, then took off. Except that just as one

Plate i

shouldn't drink and drive, neither should one drink and assume that one can run, or indeed leap, in a straight line. As I took off after my short sprint, my foot apparently struck the wall adjoining the neighbour's roof, which deflected me like a pinball machine and I went flying – or, to be most accurate, cartwheeling – off the roof.

Conversations since then have established that the lads stood for one moment not quite understanding where I'd gone – then they heard a clang. Boyfriend was rooted to the spot as his mates rushed to the edge to look down, assuming I would be lying there in the gutter of the wall in front of

---

* That's what it was called in my day. Now it's a "round-off". It comprises a run up, then a leap into a cartwheel and solid landing on both feet

the windows out of which we had climbed.

I was not there.

But thank goodness for the athletic might of my sturdy thighs – the dash across the roof had enough power to propel me far enough from the building that I missed the iron railings and the pavement (which, had I hit it, I wouldn't have survived), and landed arse first on the roof edge of a parked car. To this day I don't know who the car belonged to, but they are my salvation. And they'll be none the wiser because I didn't leave a mark on their car.

Instead, I bounced off the car and landed face first on the pavement; fracturing my pelvis in three places, fracturing a rib and puncturing a lung, knocking out a front tooth and knocking myself unconscious, a state I remained in for two and a half days.

(I had that week been doing freelance work at *Financial Times How To Spend It* magazine. The morning after my accident, when I didn't turn up for work, they called my home to find out where I was. My parents were by then sitting at my bedside in St Thomas' Hospital. My 16-year-old brother answered the phone and told the *Financial Times* – the *Financial Times*! – "Oh, she got pissed and fell off a roof. She's in hospital.")

When I woke a few days later, my consciousness returned before I opened my eyes. Not knowing where I was or what had happened, my tongue quickly encountered a chipped front tooth. I ran my tongue over it, confused. Then I opened my eyes.

Curtains were closed around my bed, and a small group of doctors stood at the foot of it, discussing my case. "Excuse me," I said. "Could I see a dentist? I seem to have lost a tooth."

Chapter Five

The day after my second consultation with Mr A, nervous exhaustion saw me falling asleep on the sofa in the afternoon. As I drifted off, the landline started ringing. Since the only people who call the landline number are my mum, my mother-in-law and Scottish Gas, I ignored it. Answering the phone would have necessitated getting up off the sofa and walking through to the kitchen, a movement for which I did not have the energy. But, having ignored the landline, my mobile phone, sitting at my head on the armrest of the chair, began buzzing angrily. This was clearly an important, if not an emergency, call. I answered the phone.

It was the genetic counselling service at hospital, offering me an appointment in three days' time. My excitement at this call was somewhat stifled by the tone of the gentleman on the other end of the line. He spoke gently, slowly and solemnly, in a manner which would have been more suited to announcing the death of a loved one. I was unnerved. When he asked if I understood the ramifications of having genetic testing for cancer, I wondered at his seriousness. The process seemed simple to me, and such sombreness unnecessary. I said yes, I understood.

No sooner had I ended the call on my mobile phone than it rang again; this time it was a young woman from the hospital calling to arrange the operation to remove my cancer two days after the genetic testing. If I hadn't been shaken awake by that call from the genetic counsellor, I certainly was now. After so much talk, my treatment would shortly be up and running. Things were starting to happen. I felt energised, excited, raring to go.

Three days later, I found myself sitting in the Genetic Services waiting room at the hospital, a full half hour early for my appointment. In this clinically dismal, square room, with only a rack of out-of-date magazines to entertain me, I lost myself in social media on my smartphone and time passed relatively quickly.

At precisely the time of my appointment the genetic counsellor picked me up from the waiting room and took me through for my consultation. It was only then that I understood the inclusion of the word counsellor in her appellation, because though I thought this appointment would entail just a blood test, said blood test actually followed 45 minutes of counselling: a rigorous recording of all known cases of cancer in my immediate family; an explanation of the BRCA 1 and 2 genes, and what the test would entail; and questions about how I would react to any given test results.

This last was the most important aspect of this counselling session. How would I feel, the counsellor asked, if it turned out I was indeed carrying a mutated gene, which I would therefore pass on to my own daughter, almost certainly resulting in her developing breast cancer as an adult? This question was apparently a crucial one, carrying possibly more significance than I gave it credit. The implication was that I should invest a lot of thought and careful consideration into the possible outcomes; but I felt they were making it more complicated than it should be.

A blood test would identify any mutations in the BRCA 1 and 2 genes; genes which produce tumour suppressor proteins. Mutations and alterations mean you're more likely to develop breast, ovarian or prostate cancer. The chances of having this mutation are extremely low but since it is inherited it would've been passed down from either my mum or my dad – would I encourage my brother to have his daughter tested? Would I encourage my cousins to be tested? How would I feel about the risk of passing the mutation onto my own daughter?

My immediate response was, surely knowledge is power? To be tested is to know the truth, to be able to access cancer screening earlier, and be in a better position to catch it and treat it. This seemed simple to me. I would rather know than not. Be in a position where I had all the facts to hand and was in control of decisions for the future. Surely that's a default position?

But no, apparently not. The medical profession especially thinks that sometimes knowledge is paranoia. And that even those who want to know maybe shouldn't. As husband pointed out, once you start worrying about inherited conditions, would you have yourself tested for all of them? The likelihood of developing diabetes? Or high blood pressure and heart disease? Or glaucoma? Well yes, why not? Then you can combat it. No, said husband. Then you just worry.

So husband understood the counselling aspect of the genetic counselling service better than I did. I just wanted to get on with it and find out.

"How are you with blood tests?" asked the counsellor as she took me through to another room for mine.

"A bit wobbly," I said, because I thought I might be. My response to needles recently had been erratic, at best. She looked concerned.

"Do you have anything with you to eat afterwards?"

"Oh no, I didn't think of that."

"You did know you'd be having a blood test?" she asked. As it happens, that's all I thought I would be having, but I hadn't paid enough attention to what that would involve. In fact, I had purposefully not thought too much about it, distracting myself by sorting the laundry. "Well, there's a place across the way that does tea and biscuits. I'll take you over afterwards." (You'll be fine if you just have tea, biscuits and a nice sit-down afterwards.)

Now I was nervous. As I lay down on the bed I chattered inconsequentially, filling the silence with high-pitched anxiety. I recalled the fraught biopsy in Tokyo (but not the successful one in Edinburgh), and convinced myself I would faint. My agitation increased when the counsellor examined the veins in the crook of my left elbow, then abandoned them to try the other arm.

"Yes," I laughed, "I have rubbish veins. A doctor once told me I couldn't be a heroin addict because I have such rubbish veins!" Please imagine the neurotic giggle that accompanied this falsetto nonsense and feel free to cringe.

But the needle's insertion into my arm was the merest scratch; and even the perhaps slightly disconcerting sound of blood squirting into a container didn't faze me. Instead, I found the sound quite fascinating.

"Well, that was easy," I said.

But the counsellor was unconvinced, probably assuming that since I had been so full of insincere bullshit in the lead up to the blood test, I was probably still full of it. She walked me out to the café across the road and saw me settled with a cup of tea and a biscuit.

Despite feeling absolutely fine, I made myself comfortable and drank the tea, which gave me space and time to ponder what had just happened. Having had the blood test, and signed the form confirming that I did indeed want to know the results, and despite the counsellor consenting to do the test, since she considered me prepared for the consequences, and despite my honestly not appreciating the potential psychological fallout from the results… I admitted to myself that I would have to think long and hard about whether my family would want to know the results.

Two days until the first operation.

Two days I crammed with laundry, tidying and cleaning. When I am nervous, I cannot control my body's production of adrenaline. I become saturated with it, which makes me anxious, edgy, breathless, prone to panic. Colours are brighter, smells more pungent. So I have learned to make good use of this energy by being constructive and doing the housework. The control freak within me is sated by drawing up to-do lists, which I tick off with smug satisfaction.

I didn't think about the operation. As far as I was concerned, there was nothing to think about. Nothing to worry about. But I was irrationally furious with the children over the slightest misdemeanour, and incandescent with rage at the builders who dropped their fag ends out their van window onto the street in front of my house.

"C*&@s!" I called them, on the phone to my mum.

"Language!" she gasped.

"My language is not as bad as their c*&@ish behaviour," I snarled. And immediately realised that of course I was worrying about the operation.

The feverish intensity reached a head on the morning of my operation, when I worked through my to-do list with an energy bordering on manic. Clothes were washed and put away, food for that evening's dinner bought, the kitchen cleaned, toys tidied away, my overnight bag packed… When I am being this ruthlessly organised, however, it is best to leave me undisturbed. I am not, generally, in the mood for being sidetracked.

Mum and dad had arrived the day before to help with the children and housework while I recovered, and mum made the mistake of interrupting my packing to ask where her gardening shoes were. I did not know where her gardening shoes were. I did not care where her gardening shoes were. Her gardening shoes were not my responsibility.

"I can cope with my to-do list but throwing your missing shoes into the mix just makes me stressed," I said. Mum nodded and smiled, knowing that her missing shoes were merely the final straw, rather than the single cause of my anxiety.

By the time mum and dad left to pick the kids up from school, and husband and I set off for hospital, I was strung to a tension so tight that if I had been strummed, the notes released would have deafened the town.

Mercifully, the tension did not spiral into an anxiety attack, as has been my wont – instead it translated into a childish excitement, a thrilling sense of adventure. I couldn't stop talking, and prattled on at speed.

Arriving at the hospital an hour early, husband and I stopped off in the nearby Holiday Inn for a cup of coffee. Well, husband had a cup of coffee, which I watched him savour, as I wasn't allowed to eat or drink anything. At least he decided against the cake, reasoning that that wouldn't be fair.

Finally, we made our way to the hospital reception, where I thought it was hilarious to announce, "Hello, I'm here for my spa treatment." Aside from the prospect of having bits chopped out of my body, this scenario was similar to a spa treatment: a night away from my children, in a room of my own, with nurses on call, a television and breakfast in bed.

But my supreme excitement about the imminent surgery was quashed by half-an-hour sitting in the waiting room, assumedly while my room was made ready. The eagerness turned into fretfulness, and I fidgeted with impatience and tension. I stared at the receptionists, attempting to call into action some sort of telepathic Jedi powers. They remained stubbornly oblivious to my silent demands to take me to my room, so I attempted to content myself by watching the comings and goings of other patients and the medical staff. Several members of the theatre staff wandered past us, in their scrubs and brightly coloured Crocs. I am not a fan of Crocs. Never have been. I think they are aesthetically ghastly and supremely impractical as footwear for children. Seeing them on the feet of the medics cemented my view of them as purely functional.

Finally, a nurse collected me from the waiting room and escorted me along the corridor to my room. As we passed through the first set of double doors, Mr A appeared like a scrubs-clad apparition, giving me quite a fright.

"Hello!" I said, my forced gaiety returning. "I'm looking forward to my massage!" I knew immediately that this was a weird thing to say, since not only had he not heard my joke about being here for my spa treatment, he would also be operating on my breast… I looked away quickly, so as not to see whatever perplexed, horrified expression he had on his face.

I had genuinely been expecting to have some sort of anxiety attack in the lead up to the operation. I have form when it comes to anxiety attacks, and had predicted the onset of a throat-constricting, finger-tingling, breath-shortening, sense-heightening, adrenaline-pumping, fight-or-flight episode.

Instead, surprisingly, I began to imagine I was on the set of *Casualty*, and hammed it up something rotten, smiling and laughing with the nurses, walking down the corridor as though I was some sort of flipping star. I enjoyed the drama. (I say this was surprising; those who know me would probably say it was par for the course.)

My room was only slightly unlike a Novotel hotel room. There were more wipe-clean surfaces. I perched on the bed and turned on the TV, while husband sat in the chair and continued working on his laptop.

A knock on the door was followed by Mr A coming in, a welcoming smile on his face. He sat on the bed next to me and explained the procedure he would be about to perform.

This would begin with a sentinel lymph node biopsy – blue dye injected into the side of the breast to indicate what path, if any, the cancer would have taken to the lymph nodes in my armpit. Those lymph nodes that turned blue would be removed for testing. Then he would slice carefully round the areola and peel back the skin to remove the cancer. Finally, he would insert a (surprisingly large) pipe into each side of my belly, remove some fat, then reinsert this fat into the now cancer-free hole in my breast. Job done.

It has to be said, I was very impressed by the process, and also by Mr A's nonchalance as he explained it. "That's just so clever," I said, which Mr A denied.

"It's really not," he said. But husband and I were adamant; I insisted it was magic, while husband was more prosaic and compared it to plastering.

"You think, that looks easy, then try to do it yourself and realise how hard it is," said husband.

"Oh, I can't do plastering," said Mr A. "Breast surgery, yes, plastering, no." I think Mr A was being unusually modest here. I think if he could perform surgery, he could probably plaster a wall. He could probably rebuild a wall. He could probably plan, design and carry out the entire construction and deconstruction of a wall, plaster it and decorate it with a fresco. Of a boob.

When Mr A confirmed which breast he would be operating on and then, with a pen, drew an arrow above it pointing down, I thought he was just displaying some sort of surgeon's gallows humour, but he told me that this was standard practice, to avoid operating on the wrong boob. I stopped laughing.

(A quick online search found the following rather worrying excerpts from *Nursing Times*[24]:

> "The incidence of surgery being performed at an incorrect anatomical site is rare (NPSA, 2005a). However, any error can be devastating and in some cases, such as the removal of a working rather than a diseased kidney, it can be fatal [!] ... However, a spot survey at a conference last year revealed that one in three theatre nurses had worked in an area where wrong-site surgery had occurred (Hartley, 2004). An NPSA investigation confirmed that wrong-site procedures occur with alarming frequency... Between November 2002 and April 2003, 15 patient safety incidents linked to wrong-site surgery were identified. Of these, three were prevented, two led to the wrong procedure and one related to intervention on the wrong side. Outcomes of the other nine were not recorded (NPSA, 2005a).")

I don't know how else a patient's bodily parts would be marked but drawing on them with an indelible pen just seemed a bit... basic.

No sooner had Mr A left us than the anaesthetist walked in, reading from his clipboard the wrong name. Bad start there. He was embarrassed and apologetic, and then began an interrogation of my lifestyle habits.

"Allergies?"

"No."

"Smoker?"

"No."

"Alcohol?"

"A lot," I said, having long ago given up memorising how many units of alcohol is considered acceptable.

"Bottle of vodka a night?" The anaesthetist joked, which lulled me into a false sense of security.

"A bottle of red," I said, truthfully.

He looked up quickly and stared at me, aghast. "Shared?!" he said, in a tone that was less a question and more a command.

Before I could calm him down with a little white lie, husband said, "I'd like to know who with. I don't get a look in."

He's a bugger.

Fortunately, the anaesthetist didn't seem to be interested in continuing with a lecture on alcohol consumption, and he left, promising that he would get my name right in theatre.

The nurse who came in shortly afterwards apologised and said that the surgery would not be for another two hours. I had already been without food for five-and-a-half hours and water for two-and-a-half. Usually such fasting would have me shaking with hunger, and with a mood to match. Luckily for husband, I now seemed to be sustained by adrenaline and a sense of adventure.

"Could you explain to me what the procedure is you're having this evening?" asked the nurse. I, thinking I was being tested, recalled what Mr A had told me, and explained the details as I remembered them.

"Did I get it right?" I asked at the end.

"Oh, yes, probably," said the nurse. "It sounds fine. I didn't know what you're having done, I hadn't been told yet." Another quick look at *Nursing Times* confirms that her questions were a test, but not for me – best practice now makes sure that patients know what will be happening to them:

> "Patients are told to expect the surgeon carrying
> out the operation to mark their skin before
> premedication or anaesthetic so that they can make
> sure the mark is in the right place. The double-
> checking system is also explained and patients are

urged to help by:
• Making sure they know what operation they are having and on which part of their body;
• Checking the surgeon's marks are in the right place;
• Telling someone if they are not sure, or think the marks may be wrong;
• Being patient with the staff asking questions as part of the checking procedure."

My knowledge of the procedure was reliant on Mr A doing his job properly.

The nurse continued with her checks: "Do you have anything in your medical history we should be aware of, anything that might have an impact on today's operation?"

The thing is, I'm not a medical expert. I didn't know what would have an impact on surgery.

"Erm… I have a numb left buttock where the nerve endings are damaged after I fell 40 feet off a roof," I proffered. How on earth I thought a numb arse would affect surgery on my breast I've no idea. But I must have thought that by giving them all the information, they could decide what to do with it.

And, ah yes. The 40-foot fall. The effect this statement usually has is to leave my audience slightly open-mouthed and asking questions. Not our young nurse, though, oh no. A 40-foot fall, you say? Pah. That's nothing.

"My dad fell off a roof!" she said excitedly. She went on to explain how her dad, working in construction in Mexico, lost his balance and fell, diving headfirst to the ground below. He managed to cartwheel midair and turn himself round just before he hit the floor, landing just on his shoulder. "His shoulder's not great but he survived!" the nurse beamed.

"I never thought wife's roof story could be bettered," said husband drily, "but you just did it."

The sense of having a spa treatment continued, as the nurse dressed me in a fetching hospital gown and a pair of sexy pressure socks (sarcasm klaxon); and then a member of the kitchen staff came in, handing me a menu and asking what I would like to eat after the operation and what I would like to have for breakfast. It was slightly surreal; the knowledge that soon I would be anaesthetised and cut open, the self-consciousness of wearing terribly unattractive clothing in front of my husband, the attention and care of the hospital staff… Like a dream sequence, these were a disjointed set of scenarios and experiences.

"Could I have a salmon sandwich after the op and lots of pastry and fruit for breakfast, please," I said as I handed back the menu. I might as well make the most of this bizarre situation.

And then it was time to settle down and pretend that nothing odd was happening, and that I wasn't worried, and this was all very normal. Which, when you're there, in that wholly new experience, you do with astonishing ease. The environment is all so civilised and humane; people know (or seem to) what they're doing. You offer up your naivety to them, and let them take control.

When the nurse returned a full half hour before I expected her I felt a small surge of nauseated agitation rotate in my stomach, but I mentally thrust that down and grinned with excitement. As I walked the corridor to theatre I smiled happily at the women on reception, feeling sorely tempted to wave. Such a drama queen.

The nurse indicated a door on my left and led me into what I thought was a walk-in cupboard, with storage on one side and a bed squeezed into the middle. A man walked in, smiling, and told me his name but not his job title so I didn't know what role he would play. One of the theatre staff I had seen in the waiting room, wearing particularly lurid Crocs, also walked in, but ignored me. I was encouraged to climb up onto the bed, all the while thinking that this couldn't possibly be the operating theatre, it was so small, and yet here we were, with theatre staff busying themselves at the counter beside me, and the nurse gently untying my gown and slipping my right arm out the sleeves, holding up a blanket to shield my body from the men.

Shield my body from the men.

This was clearly for the sake of my modesty, since I would be prone, unconscious and with a boob poking out once the anaesthetic got to work. It did seem odd to me that everyone was so precious about my privacy while I was awake. I mean, it's nice of the nurses to do that, I guess. I've heard horrible tales coming from another country I shall not name, which involved being stripped off unceremoniously and wheeled on show through the corridors.

But throughout this breast cancer treatment, male doctors had always made sure there was a female chaperone in the room while they examined me; and now the nurses held up blankets to cover me, as though my body was too precious for male eyes, as though it was too hideous to look at, as though the men would faint – or giggle – if they saw it. I wouldn't expect anything less than that, by the way – I wouldn't expect the nurses to be slapdash in their treatment of me. But I found it profoundly interesting that nobody seemed to think about telling me who would be in the room with me when I was unconscious. Why did I need protecting when awake but not when asleep?

The thing is, I am of a generation when it's not so awkward or embarrassing to have one's knockers on show. The downstairs is a bit different – in my case anyway – but boobs? I've had two children and breastfed them both. Boobs, as far as I'm concerned, are basically fleshy baby bottles, neither embarrassing nor obscene.

I would have been perfectly happy to slip out the gown in front of these medics. (Maybe that's because I'm a drama queen.)

The nurse left and the anaesthetist came in, reassuring me he had got my name right this time. The first man who had introduced himself turned out to be the anaesthetist's assistant, and they began juggling tubes, drips and stands, clattering around beside me in the small space.

I thought, this is a crazily small room for surgery. It's nothing like the operating theatres on *Casualty*. How will everybody fit in? It must be very minor surgery if it's being done in here.

A strap was tightened round my arm to encourage a bulging vein.

"Oo, there's a juicy one popping up!" said the anaesthetist delightedly.

"It's the first thing he noticed about his wife," said his assistant drily. "Her juicy veins."

The laugh that popped out of me was more of a bark. A cannula was slid easily into my wrist and taped down, and shortly afterwards the anaesthetist said, "I've just done something cheeky and given you a wee drug that'll make you feel a bit drunk."

This worried me because I get bolshy when drunk, which I pointed out. But as I gazed at the ceiling and it began to spin, I felt giggly and pleasantly dizzy. "Oo, look, yes!" I said, as though, looking up at the ceiling, the anaesthetists would also see it spinning and feel lightheaded and distant.

And then black.

The only thing I remember about waking is being back in my room and husband popping his head round the door, before coming in to sit with me.

Wait, I do remember a bit before that. I remember being awake in my room and feeling slightly confused about why husband wasn't there; slightly worried. So I asked where he was, and the nurse fetched him from the relatives' waiting room.

When he arrived I tried to speak to him but my voice was hoarse and whispering – caused by inflammation of the throat after intubation. This, too, was a surprise, my not having been warned this could happen. It's very odd when you open your mouth to speak and what comes out is not the voice you know, the voice you expect, but a harsh croak with no volume.

The shock did not turn into concern, however, since the nurse said and did nothing. If she wasn't worried, neither should I be.

I don't remember anything of what I said to husband, but I do recall being dazed and struggling to formulate words and sentences, or make sense of what I was thinking and feeling. But I wasn't too troubled by this.

Soon after, husband left and went home. I must have slept, but I woke later in the night feeling hungry, and the nurse fetched my salmon sandwich from the kitchen. An onset of nausea prevented me from finishing it, and the rest of the night passed in a hazy state of sleep and brief surfacing; woken by the nurse, who flitted in like an angel every hour to check my blood pressure, and the compression device strapped to my legs which hummed as it squeezed my calves to prevent blood clots.

At 6.30am, the drip attached to my cannula emptied itself and began beeping. I woke with a start from a sleep that had finally been deep. I pressed the button to summon the nurse, and gritted my teeth against the persistence of the beeping for another five minutes before the nurse arrived.

The drip was detached from my cannula, the stand removed and my ridiculously pastry-heavy breakfast brought through. I lay propped up on the bed, aware of the slight aching pain on my right side, a deeper, sharper pain across my belly, and a profound exhaustion. But that was it. Over. Easy.

The nurse said Mr A had called to apologise for not being able to pop in and see me; when husband arrived, he told me that after the operation he had seen Mr A, who was pleased with how things had gone, but who couldn't say until after the lump was tested if all the cancer had been removed from within its dense breast tissue.

I would have liked to thank Mr A, but as my energy returned I was keen to get dressed and return home to my children and a familiar environment. This was delayed by paperwork and admin, however; and also a brief visit from a physio (who also got my name wrong), who explained how important it was that I exercise my right arm. The lymph node excision had required a tidy slice at the base of my armpit, but I mustn't allow fear of this to stop me using that arm. I glanced at the sheet of exercises she handed to me: roll your shoulder in a circle, raise your shoulder to your ear, lift your elbow to the side… I did all that and shrugged again. I didn't know whether these exercises had been developed with older, more fragile patients in mind or the operation might have a deeper impact than I now felt.

Eventually we could leave the hospital, and I shuffled gently out of the building and climbed into the car. That journey home was pretty painful. With every bump and bounce, the spots on my stomach where pipes had been inserted and fat removed throbbed and stabbed me, reminding me of the occasions when I was in labour and husband drove me into hospital, the contractions in my belly reverberating insufferably over every pothole. I had been unprepared for this level of pain and found it slightly ironic that the surgery to remove my breast cancer had ended up causing discomfort in my stomach.

Once home, I draped myself carefully onto my bed, painkillers to hand. When the children arrived home from school, they came up to kiss me, and this was the first time that daughter properly appreciated that I was ill. To begin with, cancer is unseen. I wasn't injured or infirm. But now I was lying in bed, ostensibly unwell, and she had been told to be gentle, that she couldn't touch me, let alone hug me. I think it must have hit her then.

I Aitken

The PTSD

The impact of my illness on the children was very close to the forefront of my mind. Trauma was an experience I had already gone through and I knew its insidious and damaging effects.

To understand the concept of post-traumatic stress disorder, its history and first recordings, I did a bit of reading. Well, I started with Wikipedia[25]. Don't knock it.

I find it astonishing that the concept of a negative mental response to physical trauma became accepted, or taken seriously, only during World War One. Surely humankind had endured many centuries of traumatic experiences before then? I assume any evidence of impaired mental health would have been greeted by the accusation that it was due to a lack of moral fibre or, usually in the case of women, "hysteria". (I've just Googled "post-traumatic stress disorder and hysteria" and there are a ton of scholarly articles on the subject. Back in a minute…)

Right, so it's complicated. And the concept of PTSD was being recognised centuries ago, but wasn't properly understood.

The first real recordings of physical manifestations of mental anxiety weren't made until the 1880s, when French neurologist Jean-Martin Charcot[26] became fascinated by the "hysterical" symptoms exhibited by his patients, young women who had experienced violence, exploitation, and rape. He posited the theory that hysteria was a physical malady, not just the overemotional behaviour of weak women* – but failing to find a physical cause for this disease meant it couldn't be cured. The connection between the mental and physical was made by doctors Pierre Janet, Josef

* Interestingly, Charcot believed that men, as well as women, suffered hysteria, since, he said, it was rooted in the nervous system, not the uterus

Breuer and Sigmund Freud, who went on to show that psychological trauma caused these physical "symptoms of hysteria[27]".

Then we move on to World War One, when many doctors were convinced that the shell shock soldiers suffered was actually a physical wound; and, when this became increasingly unlikely, the British Army were damned if they were going to accept mental anguish as a proper injury…

PTSD was officially recognised as a mental health condition in 1980, when it was included in the American Psychiatric Association's Diagnostic and Statistical Manual of Mental Disorders. According to Matthew J. Friedman[28], "the significant change ushered in by the PTSD concept was the stipulation that the etiological agent was outside the individual (ie, a traumatic event) rather than an inherent individual weakness (ie, a traumatic neurosis)." PTSD symptoms[29] include flashbacks; nightmares; emotional numbing; self-blame; negative thoughts; depression; drug and/or alcohol misuse; self-harming; hyperarousal…

The reason for this very annotated history of PTSD is the fact that I had it. Or have it. I don't know if one ever becomes cured. I often feel like such a complete fraud, when I read about the sheer bloody horrors that WW1 soldiers endured; and the entirely understandable psychological impact that had. But the human mind is a fragile, little understood thing. I think we take too much for granted its ability to adjust, or ignore, or forget. It's a precious mechanism that is so easily damaged, and it is damaged, frequently, by environmental factors, by trauma, by personal tragedy… To be so damaged doesn't make the sufferer weak, or lacking in moral fibre, or hysterical, unreliable, mentally disturbed or crazy – it is evidence of their humanity. Their mortality.

There are those who might say that falling 40 feet off the roof of a building is not traumatic enough to lead to PTSD. Who am I to argue? Oh wait. I'm the person who fell 40 feet off a roof. I didn't understand the concept of PTSD, or that I might suffer it, until several years later. My own special brand of this illness was characterised by hyperarousal – feeling on edge and anxious.

No, wait.

The anxiety didn't kick in for a couple of years. What happened first was a succession of very weird symptoms which ended up making me feel as though I was going insane. One morning I woke to find a saucepan next to the bed.

"What's that doing there?" I asked. Boyfriend at the time sighed.

"You asked for it."

"What?"

"You woke in the middle of the night asking for a large bowl. I thought you wanted to be sick, but you just demanded the bowl. So I got you this saucepan, and you were fine with that and went back to sleep again."

I had no recollection of that, of course. Another night I sat bolt upright and asked,

"Are you a red lorry or a green lorry?"

"Uhhhh?" said boyfriend.

"Are you a red lorry or a green lorry?"

"What are you talking about?" asked boyfriend.

"DON'T TALK TO ME LIKE I'M STUPID!" I snapped, before falling back to sleep. Again, no recollection.

This might sound unexceptional, but I had never done stuff like this before. Sleeping is what I'm good at.

In addition, and more alarmingly, I went through a phase of just throwing up, also at night. I would wake, start an odd coughing which heralded the coming upchuck, and stomp to the loo, coughing and holding back the sick till I got there. I did this repeatedly the night before boyfriend had a job interview. He was too tired to make it. He was very annoyed.

The vomiting phase was thankfully short. But some years later, when I lived alone, the waking in the night thing restarted, this time with added hallucinations. (Some of you might be thinking that all these random side-effects sound awfully like drug-induced delirium. I honestly wasn't on drugs. Maybe a tad too much vodka, but absolutely no drugs.) One night I woke to see spiders, tens of them, scuttling up and down the wall next to my bed. Another night there were (imaginary) mice scurrying around the bedroom floor. On both occasions I was definitely awake, and I definitely saw them, but I wasn't at all bothered. I held out my hands to scoop up the creatures but when my hand touched the cold wall, or the springy carpet, the animals disappeared.

These odd manifestations of my clearly upset brain were nothing compared with the increasing anxiety that built up over the years I lived in London. This, bizarrely, occurred mostly in trains. I have no idea why. It has never been satisfactorily explained. I thought it was claustrophobia but it has been suggested by a cognitive behavioural therapist that it's more to do with a fear of lack of control after a traumatic experience.

Anyway, it started with an odd constriction of the throat. I was sitting on the train, and suddenly felt I couldn't breathe, as my throat closed over. It moved on to increased sweating, breathlessness and shaking with every journey on the London Underground, until it got to the point other passengers would blatantly avoid looking at me (this was London at rush hour. Nobody has time for someone else's breakdown), because there was clearly something wrong – I would be sitting bent over, in an attempt to draw breath, as I became light-headed and hot, my hands and feet tingling alarmingly. Finally, I couldn't even board an overland train, so overcome was I by an instinctive objection, a bodily refusal to leave the platform – of course, this was the fight or flight[30] response. If on the odd occasion I managed to step into the carriage, and the doors shut, my temperature shot up, my breathing became shallow, I became light-headed, sweaty and couldn't keep still. (Shout out to the one London commuter who spotted me panicking as the train doors shut, and sympathised without judgement across the crowded aisle. "I know, it's stressful when it's packed like this, isn't it?" she said matter-of-factly. "We'll be at the next station in a few minutes, you'll be fine." She was my saviour that day.)

I bought a car.

I did think I was going mad. I lay in bed at night, staring into the darkness, playing out the unravelling of my sanity. I was miserable. I felt like a freak.

My absolute life-saver was being referred for cognitive behavioural therapy[31]. Oh my god, was that an eye-opener. Suddenly my insanity was given a name, a justification. All those physical symptoms, I learned, were a perfectly natural result of adrenalin and cortisol release, and an (over) active nervous system. I wasn't going mad. I wasn't even abnormal. Even just the sense that I wasn't unusual, or alone, was the first step to recovery.

On the odd occasion these days that I become anxious about something,

I understand the sudden clarity of my vision, the brightness of the light and garishness of colours; I know why my sense of smell becomes so acute; I understand that if I breathe slowly, steadily and calmly, I can physically reduce the rate of my heartbeat. It's important to feel in control.

I Aitken

Chapter Six

Eight days after the sentinel lymph node biopsy and excision to remove my breast cancer, husband and I returned to Mr A for the results. We were, again, too early for the appointment, so, again, paid a visit to the nearby friendly Holiday Inn for a cuppa, which this time I could partake in, not being about to have surgery or anything.

We returned to the clinic still with time to spare – or, rather, Mr A was running late. (Appointment times were pretty abstract, and Mr A did not seem to stick to a strict schedule, preferring to spend whatever time was necessary with each patient.) I became curious about a young couple sitting nearby in the waiting room. I say curious, obviously I mean nosy. I am something of a flâneur, and am endlessly and overtly fascinated by the emotions and behaviours of other people. It's almost as though I need to learn how to behave…

Anyway, I didn't behave particularly well on this occasion, since I stared like a hawk at the clearly upset man and woman. I don't think they noticed me staring like a hawk. They were too wrapped up in their own set of circumstances, processing whatever powerful emotions they were going through. There was no interaction between the two. Nothing verbal anyway. She sat staring straight ahead, occasionally rubbing her face. He sat with one hand on her knee, gazing intently at her. When she went in to see the doctor, she went in alone, which intrigued me. (The clinic dealt not just with cancer cases, so her predicament could have been anything.) He sat waiting, his face cupped in his hands, occasionally huffing and sighing. What I wouldn't have given to be allowed to go over and comfort him and ask lots of intrusive questions. When she returned and they left together, they made it halfway across the carpark before she stopped, turned to him and tiptoed to speak into his ear. He clutched her tight to him, and then they continued. I made up all manner of stories about that expressive pair.

Despite the despondency that undulated around the young couple, when I walked into Mr A's room soon after I was grinning like an idiot. It was as though I felt a surge of post-cancer euphoria; I was frighteningly close to high-fiving Mr A.

"How are you?" he asked, with a small smile. The small smile should have rung alarm bells.

"I feel amazing," I said. "I genuinely feel so much better than I expected to. You're a magician." I was high on elation.

"You'll need to come back in for more surgery," he said. He was blunt but I was confused. What on earth damn reason was there for more surgery?

"I removed the cancer," said Mr A, smoothly and matter-of factly, "and the margins were clear." This, he said, was more difficult than usual because of my dense, "young" breast tissue, in among which it is harder to identify cancerous lumps. The margins were clear. Clear of cancer, at any rate; but two patches of DCIS[32] (pre-cancerous cells) had been identified, and they too would need to be removed. Moreover...

"The lump was 2.5cm," said Mr A, "right in the midrange where we would consider whether or not to treat with chemotherapy. But not all women are receptive to chemo, so we don't just assume you should have it." He went on to explain the concept of Oncotype[33] testing, which looks at the genomics of a cancer to see whether it would benefit from being treated by chemo. Not all cancers do. I would apparently qualify to have this testing.

But that wasn't all.

"I performed the sentinel node biopsy," continued Mr A, "when I injected blue dye into your breast to see what path, if any, the cancer would take to your lymph nodes, and I removed what I thought were three lymph nodes, but which turned out to be one lymph node and some other stuff. They tested the..."

"I'm sorry, what? 'Some other stuff'?" I interrupted him for a thorough definition of this other stuff. Said other stuff, rather than my lack of deodorant, might be the reason for the putrid odour constantly emanating from my armpit. The smell of my oxsters was such that I feared my body was rotting, or something had made its way into the wound and died.

"Fatty lobules," explained Mr A. "Lymph nodes and fatty lobules look and feel very similar. So after rummaging[*] around I removed what I thought were three lymph nodes. But there was only one. So they tested the one lymph node and found signs of micrometastases[34]– minuscule areas of cancer spread."

My oncologist (once again – I had an oncologist? Who were they? And, honestly, what was an oncologist?) had requested that Mr A remove some more lymph nodes for further testing.

"If there are no more micrometastases in the lymph nodes, you'll undergo radiotherapy – but your cancer will be sent for Oncotype testing to see whether it would be worth having chemotherapy, too," said Mr A. "And if there are more micrometastases found in the lymph nodes, you will have to have chemo anyway."

My cancer was oestrogen and progesterone receptive, aka ER+ and PR+ – that is, the cancer cells in my body were stimulated by oestrogen and progesterone. Despite Mr A maintaining that this was the most common type, accounting for 70% of all breast cancers, and was easily treated and responsive to hormone treatment, I couldn't help wonder how, since women are basically oestrogen and progesterone. To prevent the cancer, I would have to be stripped of my female hormones, right? I'd turn into a man? I didn't say any of this out loud, because I didn't know how to voice my concerns in a more sophisticated way than this, and feared being thought of as stupid and unscientific.

While attempting, and mostly failing, to process this information, I lay down on the bed to have my dressings removed and the operation site examined. I tensed as Mr A closed in to peel back the steristrips, and then yelped with pain as he did so; Mr A stepped back quickly. "I'm avoiding being punched," he grinned, but actually I think he was struck by the fetid stench of my armpit. "No wonder you made so much noise," he continued. "Look at the hair on that!" He waved the steristrips under my nose. "You've just been waxed!"

Well, thank you. Now I feel even more attractive.

The wound was pronounced well on the way to mending, and an appointment for a second excision made for two weeks' time. I felt matter-

---

[*] Yes, he said that. He "rummaged around" in my armpit. Weird

of-fact and pragmatic about this new development and laughed like a drain when husband, as we drank a glass of wine at the station waiting for our train, called these appointments our "date nights".

The next two weeks passed as a conveyor belt of timetabled normality; drudgery and regular chores overwhelmed the ability or need to worry.

When I returned for the second excision and axillary biopsy, I felt less like a TV star. Already this was a boring routine. It was certainly one that held no surprises for me, so did not necessitate childish excitement.

When Mr A joined me in my room before the op, I asked him (in all seriousness) what could be the reason for my putrid smelling armpit – had he put something in there, either by design or accident? He assured me he had smelt people much worse than me, which was something of a backhanded compliment. I also warned him that I had wind – I was genuinely afraid that he would be distracted while operating if I let rip a fart. Mr A claimed that patients don't fart under anaesthetic, which made me a little happier, though I wasn't convinced. (In fact, I'm going to look that up now…

My goodness, a lot of people have asked that question online.

And there seems to be some degree of conflict. One patient in Japan allegedly farted during surgery on her cervix, which ignited the laser being used by her surgeon[35]. But others cite "paralytic ileus[36]", which means the muscles which create the intraabdominal pressure necessary to fart are relaxed by the anaesthetic, and not working: thus, no farts. Also, since you can't eat for four hours before surgery, there won't be much gut bacteria available to cause a stink.

I feel better now.)

Mr A being required to run over the procedure again with me, I asked him a couple of questions: "So, you open up the breast and armpit in the same place as before?" I felt sorry for my newly formed scars, being forced to yield once again to the surgeon's knife. What sort of horrific welts would be left at the end of all this treatment? But yes, the wounds would be reopened. "And where the liposuction was before, does the pipe go back into those holes?" I didn't want to have multiple circular scars over my stomach but at the same time, I dreaded recreating the pain of the first surgery. But no, said Mr A, I wouldn't be having liposuction at all.

My breast was far too tender after the previous surgery to have yet more fat pumped into it. It was still swollen, which would make it unclear how much fat needed to be deposited there.

I was at first perturbed by this news – I had been expecting liposuction. Part of me looked forward to having just a wee bit more fat removed from my chubby tummy. I also didn't want to end up with a right breast markedly smaller than the left.

"The cancer I removed last time was 20g," added Mr A, apropos of nothing, "and the amount of fat I injected in there was 130g."

A 20g tumour! That's the same as… 20g of sugar. (An AA battery weighs 24g, so my cancerous mass weighed a little less than a battery.) And the amount of fat taken from my belly and squeezed into that 20g cavity was equivalent to… 130g of flour! Or a half baguette. Though not, I hope, the same shape.

How was it that a fat mass more than six times the weight of the cancer could be squeezed into the same hole? I know that Mr A would have removed as little healthy breast tissue as possible. Treatments for breast cancer nowadays are much more delicate and non-invasive than they used to be. I can only conclude that fat is, indeed, heavy stuff.

Returning to the conversation about liposuction, Mr A did not yield to my insistence on having it, for which I am grateful. Lord knows my poor body was being battered enough as it was, without pipes being reinserted and body tissue being sucked out and squeezed in again.

Another question; one which had been bothering me to some degree. Was all this treatment worth it? Would it entirely destroy all remnants of cancer from my body? "Could my cancer metastasise? Spread to another part of my body some years from now?"

"Yes," said Mr A. "That is always a possibility. But that's why we carry out treatments such as hormone therapy, chemo and radiotherapy – to reduce the risks. But there is always a risk of any disease occurring." I'm not sure that deep down I was totally comforted by this. Yes, there is no point worrying about that which is beyond one's control. Scientists and surgeons might be godlike in their abilities but no-one and nothing can truly control death and disease. That's down to Mother Nature. (And, despite the implications of her maternal moniker, she's not always particularly nurturing.) But in that hospital room, listening to my consultant's pragmatism, I shrugged and nodded my agreement, as much to persuade myself that I wouldn't waste my energy worrying.

Following Mr A was the anaesthetist, a different one from my first surgery. This one spoke so fast I stopped listening and trying to understand what he said; I was bewitched by the velocity of his speech. I watched his face like a hawk, seeking signs of breathing between the stanzas.

"Hi, I'll be asking questions and having my head down and filling in the form, sorry to be rude, smoker? Allergies? Alcohol?" I could barely register each question, let alone answer it before he was on to the next one. With the absence of eye contact, I became fascinated by his accent, and attempted to place it. When he had gone I discussed it with husband, and we agreed we thought it was Birmingham, or thereabouts.

When it was time for my surgery, I walked quietly along the corridor – I didn't feel the need to wave at the staff on the nurses' station, or at an imaginary paparazzi. I wasn't buzzing with nervous excitement; I was resigned and meek.

I say meek. Actually, not having eaten for nearly eight hours, I was shaking with an almost feral hunger, and eyed with barely concealed starvation the kitchen staff member who shared the lift up to the first floor while balancing three plates of sandwiches in his hands. He smiled thinly.

And, of course, when we turned left off the corridor, this time I knew that the walk-in cupboard we entered wasn't the operating theatre, but the anaesthetic room. I don't know at what point this realisation had hit me but it was slightly reassuring knowing that my surgery would not, after all, be performed in this tiny room of cupboards and drip stands.

With my new-found ennui brought on by experience, I climbed onto the bed and removed my arms from the gown sleeves, while Dr Q the anaesthetist held up the blanket to preserve my modesty. I have no modesty. It was pretty unnecessary.

When it came to Dr Q inserting the cannula into the back of my hand, he struggled to locate the vein, since I hadn't had anything to drink for four hours and my vein had all but sunk from trace. I felt the pinching and scraping of the needle under my skin and wriggled with discomfort.

"This is a good effort," said Dr Q's assistant. "Normally he takes loads more goes than this." I thought that next time I would ask for the cannula to be inserted in my wrist, as it had been for my first procedure, rather than my hand; and then I laughed inwardly that I was assuming there would be a next time.

"What's your accent?" asked Dr Q. "I've been trying to place it."

"Sussex; I'm from near Brighton," I said, as Dr Q and his assistant shuffled around me, organising drips and tubes. Then I made the mistake of hazarding a guess at his own accent, and repeated what husband and I had concluded earlier. "You're from the Midlands?"

Dr Q took a sharp intake of breath and pouted crossly.

"Manchester!" he spat, and I was mortified, because everyone can recognise a Manchester accent. And even if you can't, it sounds nothing like a Midlands one. Here was me accusing him of being a Brummie, and he was in charge of my anaesthetic.

But clearly he was a man of principle, because almost immediately the ceiling began to spin and I was thrust into blackness.

I woke in the recovery ward, and this time was aware of it; aware of the two rows of beds, with bodies prone and quiet, and nurses bustling among them. "Well, hello!" said one. Nurse that is, not prone body. None of those was in a fit state for conversation. And neither was I, so I didn't respond and merely gazed around me, groggy and apathetic. I was eventually wheeled back to my room, where husband joined me – but when I tried to speak I realised there was still an oxygen mask covering my face.

"Your blood oxygen levels are still a bit low," explained the nurse, "so we just need to get your saturation levels up a bit." I had a twinge of worry at this, which was quickly deadened by post-anaesthesia ennui.

When husband left, I dozed and woke, dozed and woke – I was groggy but not as knocked out as I had been after the previous operation, probably because this time the procedure had not involved liposuction. I felt less pain, and was slightly more alert.

"Erm, do I not have to wear that compression thing?" I asked the nurse, pointing to my legs. "Not that I want to tell you how to do your job!" The nurse disappeared and returned with the intermittent pneumatic compression device, wrapping it round my legs and switching it on to release its incessant buzzing and regular squeezing of my lower legs. I immediately regretted having said anything.

A second nurse entered soon after and informed me that she would inject an anti-coagulant into my stomach. My stomach! I felt slightly nauseated with fear at the discomfort this would cause and expressed my concern. "It'll be sore, won't it?"

"Yes," said the nurse. "It is very sore, and it really stings. But I would have it." That immediately swayed me. If a member of the medical profession would voluntarily have such treatment, it must be good enough for me. I pulled up my gown.

The nurse leaned over me and almost immediately stepped back. I looked at her and realised she had injected me and I had felt nothing – then a slight fizzing sting bubbled up and ebbed away.

"Ah," I said. "That didn't hurt at all."

"It's called reverse psychology," said the nurse. I call it taking the piss, but it worked, so.

Unlike the night after my first operation, I slept very little from then on. I was hot, sweaty, uncomfortable, fidgety, and there were a couple of patients in other rooms nearby who regularly and noisily vomited through the night. I eventually fell asleep at about 2.45am – and was woken at 6am by the hospital coming to life, nurses speaking at daytime volume, trolleys being trundled down the corridor. I got up and changed into pyjamas, opening the curtains to a beautiful sunny day, feeling – though tired – relatively sanguine.

A pot of tea was brought into my room, and the angel bearing it asked me what my pain was like, on a scale of 1 to 10. I immediately plumped for 1, then asked if they would accept 0.5. I don't know what sort of morphine they had had me on, but it was going above and beyond in its role as a painkiller.

When breakfast – melon salad and a pain au chocolat – arrived an hour later I couldn't have felt more like I was being brought room service in a hotel. Albeit a hotel with wipe-clean lino flooring and a narrow bed on wheels.

When husband arrived to take me home, the nurse insisted I take with me some stronger analgesics than before, since I had had a re-excision, and the wound would probably feel more sore. So instead of paracetamol and ibuprofen, which had done me just fine the last time, I was provided with paracetamol and dihydrocodeine for the pain and diclofenac to reduce the swelling. As it turned out, she was quite right – there was more discomfort, and I was glad to have more hardcore painkillers to deal with it. I was also glad not to have the bruising and swelling on my stomach to contend with.

Only a few hours after I arrived home from hospital, I received a call from the genetic counselling service – the results of my blood test were in, and I did not have any BRCA gene mutations. This was obviously a relief – it meant I would not immediately need to have the aggressively invasive treatment that was a mastectomy, and I would not need to have my ovaries removed as a preventive measure. More importantly, it meant I would not need to be concerned about my daughter's future health, or persuade my cousins and brother to have themselves and their children tested. There was no need to spread panic.

"I would say, though," added the counsellor, "looking at your family history, the female relatives on your mum's side would qualify for breast cancer screening from the age of 35, rather than the usual 50."

I ended the call with a sense of relief – but also with a pang of guilt that I hadn't been more assiduous about my own screening. If I had made sure to continue with the mammograms, this cancer might have been caught all the sooner.

A week and a half later I was back in clinic for the second boob op results. The wait in the waiting room was always a silent one. There were invariably other patients and their partners waiting alongside us, to see my or another consultant or nurse. But small talk was in low tones, and conversation among the patients was non-existent. Why this would surprise me, I don't know – one rarely encounters conversation in a doctor's waiting room, unless it's among people who know each other. For some reason, this clinic I thought would be different – perhaps because of the heightened emotion engendered by the reasons for being there. Of course, I couldn't have known all the reasons for people being there, but judging by the headscarves and hair shortage, there were certainly a few cancer patients among them. But the surroundings were hardly conducive to cocktail-evening chatter – the room didn't share the drab browns and beiges that hide a multitude of sins in a standard doctor's surgery, but the blunt turquoise of the walls was certainly nothing but clinical.

Perhaps it was nervous adrenalin that always fuelled my desire for gossip and laughter. I had to make do with wittering in whispers to my husband.

"How did that last operation go for you?" asked Mr A when we trooped into his room. I drew a breath as I gathered my thoughts, but he continued, "I think it all went very well."

"Do you want to hear my answer?" I asked bluntly. DE, the chemo nurse associated with Macmillan Cancer Care, was sitting quietly and calmly behind Mr A, and her maternal expression turned to one of matriarchal delight at my tone.

"Oh, yes, of course," said Mr A, awkwardly.

To be honest, my answer was very dull, so I shouldn't have been surprised that he might want to gloss over it. But I felt a subconscious need to unburden myself, to file and diarise my experience out loud, to document the ordeal for the man who was responsible.

"It must have been a quicker procedure? Using less anaesthetic? I woke earlier and was more alert all night. But I have felt slightly more uncomfortable while recovering – I came off the painkillers after a few days but had to go back on them because it was all quite sore."

Mr A nodded, but I felt his nodding was more an acknowledgement that he had heard me say something, rather than any real interest in what I had been saying.

I now wonder if my verbal diarrhoea was less a need to process the information swilling round in my head and more a delay tactic, preventing him from delivering his verdict.

"You will have to come back for more surgery," he said smoothly, and then left a silence while I thought about what he had said.

"Were the margins not clear?" I asked.

"Oh no, I removed all the cancer from your breast. But the three lymph nodes I managed to remove from your armpit are cancerous."

"More micrometastases?" I asked, savouring the medical linguistics.

"No, proper cancer. So you will need to have chemotherapy."

The following 20-minute conversation was almost white noise to me. I nodded with feigned understanding as Mr A outlined the treatment process I would go through that summer. Fortunately, husband took notes and asked apposite questions. I made quips and stayed cynically straight-faced.

My schedule now looked like this:

 • A CT scan and bone scan in the next week

• A meeting with my oncologist (finally! I would meet them!) to discuss my chemo regimen
• A course of chemotherapy
• A final operation to remove all the lymph nodes from my right armpit (a precautionary and preventive measure)
• A course of radiotherapy.

Mr A told me it was a lot to take in, and that the emotion that was no doubt engulfing me inside would surface soon. I took this as though it were an accusation. I was almost offended by his assumption that I was weak, emotional, that I was putting on this calm facade. He didn't know me. He didn't know how I responded to crises. I felt proudly freakish that apparently I wasn't reacting like all his other patients.

But I don't think, now, that my calm demeanour was due to unusual strength of character; I think it was because I genuinely didn't understand the impact all this would have. It was a to-do list, not an interactive moment when I could see, hear, feel all that I would go through. So I'm handed a list of treatments; so what? It's just a ton of information. It's a glut of data I have to go away to process; I have to take time to assimilate. To indulge in histrionics then and there, with the news that I would have to go through many months of treatment before I was truly rid of cancer, would have been phoney. Forced. Because I was far from emotional. I was blank.

At home, as I allowed myself to think more about what chemotherapy meant, I pictured myself lying on the sun lounger in our sunny back garden, with books and a sick bucket to hand. My understanding was that there would be nausea and tiredness. It was a two-dimensional understanding, a warm, colourful, almost idyllic image.

I Aitken

The Caffeine

S uch a naive understanding of what was to come could well have been my brain's way of neutralising fear – a method of side-stepping the anxiety attacks I had suffered in my late twenties.

Then, mum became convinced that these occasional anxiety attacks were down to too much caffeine. This was not as far-fetched a theory as you might think – she had developed a caffeine intolerance herself when she was in her 30s. Having drank coffee most of her adult life, she suddenly started having bouts of very high heart rates and nausea when she drank a cup. She laid off the stuff and never had a funny turn again (until she was given a fully caffeinated coffee by accident and was struck down).

I didn't entirely dismiss this idea, but was pretty sure that my anxiety attacks were exactly that – anxiety attacks, rather than an allergy or food intolerance. After all, I had suffered a plethora of exciting PTSD side effects over the years. Surely this was just another one?

My stimulant of choice for deadline weeks at work was Dr Pepper. How I loved Dr Pepper. Its cherry-esque* caramel sweetness fizzed down my throat, when the 42.6mg/12oz[37] caffeine content then warded off sleepiness and kept me alert and on my toes.

But this high-octane acuity, this feeling of adrenaline-fuelled energy, subsided into a more frequent queasiness and uncomfortably fast heartbeat. I began to wonder if mum was right after all. I decided to lay off the Dr Pepper.

And then I had a paracetamol "plus" variety. I didn't realise – but you probably know – that usually a painkiller labelled "extra" or "plus"

---

* Apparently some people think it's almond/marzipan. Whatever

means it is laced with caffeine, which raises blood pressure and increases heart rate, allowing the painkiller to travel round your body and quell discomfort faster than normal.

Well, I had a headache. A pretty standard, dehydrated work-stress headache. I took a paracetamol "plus". And then I thought I was going to die.

There went my heart rate, becoming faster and faster, pounding against my chest; there went my breathing, shallow and rapid. I couldn't keep still, had to stand, then walk, then run down the stairs to the toilets in the basement, stare at my frightened reflection in the mirror there…

I ran back up to reception and sat with my hands on my knees, trying to loosen my chest enough to draw a long, lung-filling breath. The receptionist asked if I was okay. "I think I'm dying," I said, not at all over-dramatically. He called an ambulance.

I had to go outside to wait, I couldn't stay indoors any longer, I needed fresh air, a sense of space. When the ambulance arrived, I can't remember what I told the paramedics – that it could be either a panic attack or a reaction to caffeine. They sat me in the back of the ambulance and checked my pulse.

"You have a resting heart rate of 143bpm. That's pretty high," said a paramedic. They advised me to go to Kingston Hospital, and started to prepare for the journey. But my heart banged painfully fast in my chest, as I glanced around the ambulance's small cabin.

"I can't travel in here!" I panicked, claustrophobia spilling out of me and filling the space. "Does the window open?" The paramedics, with no discussion or argument, suggested I sit in the front passenger seat. On the journey, they explained that this was usually absolutely against all protocol.

"Won't you get into trouble?" I asked.

"You couldn't travel in the back and we need to get you to hospital," they shrugged. These guys have the most amazing capacity to think on their feet. I love them all.

Once in triage, clearly not an emergency, I sat in the waiting room for an hour or so, and eventually saw a doctor. She diagnosed a panic attack, though I did bring up the subject of caffeine intolerance. I left, much calmer but so mortified – nobody had berated me for wasting NHS time and money, yet that's what I had done. Again.

I avoided caffeine – including tea – for the next 14 years, though recently have experimented with the odd Coke or latte. No more attacks yet. The cause of those before remains unproven.

I Aitken

Chapter Seven

That idyllic image of resting in the back garden in between chemo sessions got me through several days – days of otherwise pretty blank, neutral emotion. I was clearly in shock, though I didn't feel it at the time. I thought I was being cool and in control. But that's the wonder of the human brain, which knows better than you do what you can cope with and what you can't, and puts up barriers to protect you from the sensation of trauma.

After a few days of relative calm, my brain seemed to think I could tolerate a few home truths, and slowly allowed the deeply submerged emotions to seep out.

The first thing I did was burst into tears when I realised I had thrown away all the get well cards I had received thus far. Why on earth did I do that? (I kept all the cards from then on.) Because I thought that after two operations, that was the end of the cancer, that's why. The end of the illness, the end of having to think about it. I am a ruthless binner of ephemera, the opposite of a hoarder (unless we're talking books and shoes), and when I saw what I thought was the end of my illness, perhaps I didn't want to see any more reminders that I had been ill. I was unsparing. Cold. Those beautifully tailored, personal, heartfelt messages, all swept into the recycling box of doom. What. A. Bitch.

And it all went pretty much downhill from there, as I crashed to the ground from a cloud of indifference. Thoughts of mortality were ever-present, and with them throat-hardening, choked-back tears. I peaked and troughed, between sensibly planning for my death (ie, realising the need to close my bank account, cash-in my ISA, update my will, etc) and then panicking about who would look after my children when I had gone. I looked back over my own life and my self-judgement was eviscerating

– I had been a rubbish daughter, I told myself, an unreliable friend, an unambitious worker, a selfish hedonist. I didn't go so far as to say I deserved to die, but I certainly didn't feel as though I would be a great loss to anyone.

Apart from my children, of course.

Before the Brexit vote – stay with me – husband and I had talked about the possibility of moving to mainland Europe; perhaps Germany? Or maybe just Ireland? After the Brexit vote, expressing his disappointment and disbelief in the result, husband returned with surprising enthusiasm to the idea of moving abroad. I was delighted, being at heart an itinerant; a footloose, easily bored rolling stone. But now I was ill, possibly dying (no, no, not at all overdramatic), I couldn't bear the thought of my babies cut loose from all their friends and family, forging their way in foreign lands, cultivating new friendships while their dad worked. Terrified and close to tears (yet again), I begged husband to stay put. Well, begging was unnecessary, obviously. He didn't need to put much thought into the idea of moving our young children to a foreign country after I died, and having to raise them among strangers while he also worked; he agreed to stay put. But my fears and simmering panic were gradually building to a level where they were having an impact on my health and happiness each day; I watched videos of CT and isotope bone scans (which I would shortly be having), and felt physically sick at the mere thought of having to lie still and alone in a room of cold, metal machinery. My claustrophobia waved at me. "*Hello! Remember me? Yes, you will be overcome by my gripping tentacles while going through this process! You'll get clammy and short of breath and incapable of staying still!*"

With rising hysteria, I shared my fears with husband. He gently reminded me of the diazepam I had taken with me to Japan, to ease the long-haul flights. My heart slowed down. I sat still. I smiled. Of course. Diazepam.

On the morning of my CT scan, I first drove to the Maggie's Centre[38], a small, many-windowed, brightly sunlit building nestling next to the hospital. Maggie's Centre offers a wealth of free services, including relaxation and yoga classes, support groups, one-on-one psychology sessions, and also visits from the Look Good Feel Better[39] volunteers, who do wonders showing how to tie a headscarf and paint on such necessary facial furniture as eyebrows.

I heard of Maggie's Centre through a friend who had worked there – she had urged me to make use of its facilities, but I didn't understand what it could do for me. I found out as soon as I walked through the door. I was greeted with kindness, and sat in a comfy chair with a biscuit and a cup of tea, before a psychologist joined me to listen to my worries. She was calm and soothing, her expression unperturbed and unjudgemental. There was no awkwardness. I found it easy to talk to her because I felt as though that was what she was there for – to listen. She explained what to expect from the process I would go through, and explained how I would probably feel – but with none of the patronising tone that assumed knowledge of who I was. She also explained how I was allowed to feel, which released a valve that had, quite unknown to me, been suppressing my very deepest fears.

There is the odd daily wobble when you're unwell, the fear occasionally surfacing with a need for hugs and a few silent tears. But much of the deeper agitation is pushed down, locked away, hidden behind a mask – no-one wants to see abject illness, or terror, or depression. There is a duty to be brave. Cancer patients are constantly greeted with the expression that they are "bravely battling" their illness. It's an expression that has always pissed me off. Not only is it untrue – having cancer is pretty much a passive exercise; it's the surgeons who battle it, not the patient, so if anyone should be blamed for "losing" the battle, it's them – it also sets an impossibly high bar that all cancer patients must live up to. What if you're not brave? What if you're terrified? What if you cry all the time? Well, you can't, because cancer patients are obliged to be "brave", not scared and cowardly. So those deeper, darker emotions are kept hidden as best they can be – until the Maggie's Centre psychologist allowed me those feelings, those fears; understood them, verified them, gave them credence.

Oddly enough, rather than then be overwhelmed by a tsunami of black thoughts, I had something of an epiphany. With the realisation that I was entitled to be distressed, I suddenly realised that of course I could not control my mortality. No-one can. But though I could not take charge of my cancer or steer away from my death, I could control my life; how

I lived around and in between the illness and its treatments. This was a revelation, leading to such a sense of relief and new power, and I left Maggie's Centre lighter and happier.

Early for my CT scan at the clinic, I made my customary visit to the nearby Holiday Inn and, mindful of impending anxiety, ordered a cup of chamomile tea. Honestly, does chamomile tea really have soothing properties? Is it maybe more a placebo? Anyway, between the counselling at Maggie's Centre and this hot mug of herbal tea, I felt positively serene in the clinic waiting room – until the pained screams and shouts of a woman, presumably a patient, echoed up the corridor.

"Don't worry," laughed the receptionist, "she's not having what you're having!" Not helpful.

When a nurse brought me the one-litre jug of "aniseed-flavoured water" I was told was necessary to drink before my CT scan, I also popped a couple of diazepam. This aniseed drink, a litre of which I had to drink in the 45 minutes before my scan, was an x-ray dye which clarifies images of the bowels and intestines. I gallantly set to sipping cups of the stuff, a task that wasn't too arduous since I like aniseed. Another woman in the waiting area was having to work her way through two litres of something she said tasted of metal. She was struggling.

When I was taken through to the scanning area to change into a gown, I took deep breaths and was thankful that I had popped those pills, instead of relying on the unproven chamomile. Until I saw the CT scanner, which wasn't so much a room of cold, metal machinery as an upright doughnut. I was happily underwhelmed.

As I lay on the bed, the radiographer inserted a cannula in my right arm. "We'll be injecting a contrast dye," she said. "This could make you feel as though you're having a hot flush, but that'll only last a minute or two. You could also get a metallic taste in your mouth, and the sensation that you've peed yourself."

A sudden fear suffused me.

"What if I do pee myself?" I asked.

"Then you'll set a precedent," she replied. That was no comfort.

I knew immediately the dye was injected because I was suddenly very hot, my mouth flooded by the taste of metal and my groin warm enough to feel as though I'd wet myself. (Come on, we all know that feeling, don't deny it.) I laughed with incredulity that such a response is so universal and predictable.

When the radiographer left the room, the doughnut began a loud humming, "like an aeroplane", the radiographer had said, but I thought it was more of an angry washing machine. My bed slowly slid back and forth through the doughnut, a recorded voice telling me when to hold my breath and when I could release it. Three minutes later the radiographer returned to the room and told me it was over. I left the clinic feeling both smugly satisfied that I hadn't panicked and slightly embarrassed that I had taken drugs to hold the panic at bay, in what was essentially a stress-free experience. (Hmm. Chicken and egg scenario, though. Was it stress-free because I had taken the drugs?)

The next day was the isotope bone scan, in the larger city hospital. I made my way through the crowds to the x-ray department, and sat in the big, beige, windowless waiting area, a soulless and depressing space. This was not a busy area – a few medical staff stood at the reception desks talking quietly; a couple of other patients wandered in and took seats as far apart from one another as possible; the air was heavy with that windowless room's timeless, oppressive suffocating blanket of an atmosphere. I couldn't work in that sort of environment.

Husband arrived just as the radiographer came to collect me. My usual ire at husband's characteristic tardiness had been smothered by a couple of those diazepam pills (which I had consumed to stave off panicking during the bone scan, not to calm me down in case husband was late. Though, actually, that might be a good idea), so I smilingly handed husband my bag and followed the radiographer to a small room, where he placed on the desk a metal box displaying the radioactive icon.

I grew unfeasibly excited at this development. I felt like something out of a Marvel film, as he drew on gloves and prepared the radionuclide[40] syringe. This was a radioactive liquid which would travel through my blood stream and gather in my bones, pooling in larger quantities in areas of bone damage or cancer, which pooling would then be picked up by the gamma camera of the machine I would be slid through. So, for the next few hours, I would be actually, physically radioactive. Considering I have an entirely rational fear of all things nuclear and radioactive, I was stupidly exhilarated by this process. I love science, me.

The radionuclide liquid having been deposited in my blood stream, I was instructed to entertain myself for three hours, and to drink 1.5 litres of water in that time, allowing the fluid to spread throughout my body. I was told to avoid prolonged contact with small children and pregnant women – I didn't ask how small a small child was – which proved amusingly difficult as we whiled away the time in the café and lobby areas of the hospital. "Amusingly" because I enthusiastically took on the role of radioactive super villain, and theatrically jumped aside every time I encountered someone who might be susceptible to my atomic venom. Oh, how we laughed.

Three hours later I returned to the x-ray department and was instructed to empty my bladder of those 1.5 litres of water. (Which, now I think of it, seems a little odd. Why did they want me to drink so much liquid if all I was going to do was pee it straight out again before the scan? Ours not to reason why, I suppose.) This I had to do in a special toilet for radioactive people, so as to avoid the possibility of contaminating mere mortals with my glowing pee.

When I was shown into the scanning room, those little diazepam pills stood me in good stead, because this time, unlike for the CT scan, there was no jolly-looking doughnut. This time there really was a big metal contraption, into which I would be slid on a bed. A bed I was strapped onto. Also, and I knew this before the radiographer warned me, thanks to my nervous and assiduous internet research, during the scan a metal plate would lower to a point just above my nose, just in case I wasn't feeling claustrophobic enough.

So, feeling a false calm induced by prescription drugs, I lay still as my arms were strapped by my side, the radiographers left the room, and the bed slowly slid into the machine. I closed my eyes and began to breathe deeply and slowly. Then I opened my eyes – and gazed straight up at a shiny metal plate, mere centimetres from my nose. I shut my eyes again quickly and commenced the counting. I managed to count to 500 before I drifted off into a semi-conscious state; and then woke with a visible start when the radiographer came into the room and cheerily called out, "Right, that's it then!"

"You gave me a fright!" I said. The scan had taken 20 minutes – once again I left the hospital with a huge sense of relief that it was over, and that it had not been half as bad as I had feared.

My first appointment with my oncologist (I was finally going to meet her!) was later that evening, making going home and returning almost immediately to the city pretty pointless. So, since all these appointments had taken on a date night quality, husband and I stayed in the city and he treated us to a slap-up meal in a posh restaurant. Aware that the imminent meeting with my oncologist would signal the beginning of a pretty shite summer, and that the CT and bone scans could reveal whether the cancer had spread further, I savoured every taste, sight, smell and sound. I smiled at husband and gazed out the window at the warm evening sky, an ochre blue backdrop to Edinburgh Castle's highland mountain brown and grey silhouette.

My plebeian habit of earwigging on other diners' conversations*, however, was disappointed by the nearest table being occupied by a group of Spaniards. The sum total of my Spanish is *por favor* and *graçias*, so I didn't get much out of listening to them. Instead I had to listen to husband.

On the way to the clinic, I wondered whether my oncologist would be the incredibly stylish blonde woman I had occasionally seen passing through the waiting room. Nurse DE had told me that Dr B was ridiculously glamorous and everyone at the clinic was in love with her. It transpired that Dr B was indeed the blonde woman – a chic young Greek Consultant Medical Oncologist and Clinician Scientist in Breast Oncology, with an impressive trail of medical qualifications and an astonishing aptitude for unsmudged feline eye liner.

"She is lovely," I mouthed at DE over Dr B's shoulder.

"Ssshhhh!" DE mouthed back.

Sat in Dr B's room, I began the conversation. "DE says you won't have the bone scan results until tomorrow."

"That's right, but I'm confident it will be clear as the CT scan was clear," said Dr B with an insouciance that stopped me in my tracks.

"Was it?"

---

* Don't judge me. One learns an awful lot about humanity and the problems we face from idle chat in restaurants and cafés

"Oh. They didn't tell you?" asked Dr B, again with a nonchalance that was almost infuriating.

"No."

"Well I'm telling you — the CT scan is clear," said Dr B, her off-handedness implying that of course the scan was clear. Why wouldn't it be?

I sat in relieved silence as Dr B went on to outline my programme of chemotherapy. I would receive ECT: epirubicin and cyclophosphamide together every two weeks for four cycles; then Taxol every week for 12 weeks. That was 16 weeks of treatment. Four months of my life given over to having toxins pumped into my body.

Dr B's blasé matter-of-factness continued with her assurance that yes, I would experience hair loss and nausea with the EC drugs, but there would be no side effects from the Taxol — an assertion somewhat undermined by the leaflet she handed me... which listed all the side effects of Taxol.

But Dr B's supreme serenity was very heartening, and I left her office with the feeling that even if everything wasn't under my control, it was under Dr B's and the team of chemo nurses who would be treating me. She had sounded very much as though she knew what she was talking about, which is pretty much what a patient wants to hear in their doctor. I left smiling, and almost overtaken by the urge to hug her, except that I didn't dare crumple her sophistication with my enthusiasm.

And the next morning, Dr B called to let me know that the bone scan was also clear — the cancer had not spread further than the lymph nodes in my armpit. All I would need to obliterate all signs of the illness would be a course of chemo, one last operation and a blast of radiotherapy.

Ha.

Now, of course, with this good news, my brain decided that it would be okay to release all my suppressed fears. It did so in a none too subtle way, and I spent the next couple of days overreacting to everything my family said and did, taking all comments personally and crying uncontrollably. This is the "bravery" of the cancer patient.

In the short period before my first chemo session, there were several things that needed to be done: flu and pneumococcal jabs; a minor operation to insert a portacath into my chest; and daughter's 7th birthday, with associated party.

Attempts to organise the flu and pneumococcal jabs were somewhat beset by a farcical chain of events. They would be necessary because chemotherapy destroys white blood cells, so my immune system needed to be given a fighting chance against common illnesses. But I was in need of these jabs out-of-season — apparently nobody gets flu in May. I was being desperately unfashionable.

Which meant that, when I called the GP's surgery, I was told there were no flu vaccinations in stock, and that I would need to source some from a chemist. I called the local chemist, who said they had none, but the larger store 40 miles away might. I called the larger store 40 miles away, who confirmed that yes, they did have the flu vaccination in stock, and I could come and get it. And then I received a call from my local GP, saying that the clinic did have flu vaccinations in stock after all, and all this phoning around was entirely unnecessary. I bit the telephone. I made an appointment for the jabs.

And then I made some nervous calls to ask when I might be having the operation to insert a portacath* — aka implantable port — in my chest, since I would be starting chemotherapy, like, quite soon, and would need a means of receiving it. (The port is a little device that sits just under the skin, with a thin tube, also under the skin, running from the port to a vein near your heart.) I was assured that all was under control and I would receive a call with a date for the minor op very soon.

They told no lies. The call came shortly afterwards, and an appointment for the port op was made for two days later.

Two days later was daughter's seventh birthday.

Accordingly, alarm clocks were set for a ridiculously early hour that morning, so that daughter could open her presents. She seemed admirably unfazed that her birthday was being undermined by my treatment. Knowing her as I do, this would have been because she was at least being given gifts. Daughter can be assuaged by all things that are plastic crap.

---

* A portacath is a small device that sits under the skin of your chest. A tiny tube leads from the device to a vein close to your heart. When you need treatment, a needle is pushed into the device to deliver the chemotherapy drugs from a drip. The drugs travel from the device through the tube and into your bloodstream. The portacath stays in place for as long as you need treatment[41]

Present giving and the school run complete, husband drove us to the hospital.

My third time in this hospital. To say it felt like home would be stretching it a bit but I did walk into my room and throw my bag on the bed with a large degree of familiarity. The kitchen staff came to take my post-lunch order, which I delivered with practised nonchalance. (Inside I was still thinking, this is such fun! It's like being in a hotel!) Then the anaesthetist and surgeon joined me to explain the procedure. The anaesthetist was a lovely, warm, twinkly-eyed man, into whose hands I immediately entrusted myself. The surgeon was a very jolly-hockey-sticks persona, ebullient and cheerful. The anaesthetist explained that I would be having a local anaesthesia under sedation, since there would be a degree of digging around in my chest and it would be best to have me high-as-a-kite in that situation. He didn't put it like that.

"Once I'm into things, I won't chat much," said the surgeon. "But just let the anaesthetist here know if there's anything you need." *Like what?* I thought. *A gin and tonic? A foot massage?*

They left, and shortly afterwards a nurse collected me from my room and led me to theatre — a different one from my previous two operations. I was led through the anaesthetist's room — a different walk-in cupboard, this one larger than before, where the anaesthetist, wearing a very snazzy surgical cap, greeted me — and straight through into theatre. Aha! This is an operating theatre! I thought. Much roomier and more like the sets on *Casualty*. Again, as the theatre staff gently ushered me into place, I felt like a celebrity; so special.

Lying on the bed in the centre of the room, I had a small sheet placed above my face so I wouldn't be able to see what was going on in my chest. The anaesthetist first injected me with a sedative. "Feeling anything yet?" he asked.

"Nope," I said, I hoped clearly and emphatically enough for him to do something about it. And then, and I have no idea quite what happened, I found myself staring at him, thinking nothing.

"Anything now?" he asked. I heard him speak. But not only could I say nothing back, I didn't want to. Wide-eyed and blank, I gazed at his smiling face. "I think that's you," he laughed.

For the next half hour, I was snug in a sedated cocoon, aware of but not responsive to the rummaging and gentle poking in my chest. In retrospect, it is a very weird state to be in — to all intents and purposes fully conscious, but unresponsive, apathetic. Of course, while you're in it it doesn't feel weird at all. It just feels… nice. Calm. Almost blissful.

Once the port and wire were in place, I was wheeled back to my room to wait for the cocoon of indifference to gently fall away. Then it was a quick sandwich and straight back home, followed by a jaunt to the GP clinic that afternoon for the flu and pneumococcal jabs.

"I had the port put in this morning!" I told the nurse, waving in the general direction of my dressings and expecting her to be just as amazed as I was that I had undergone minor surgery just hours before, and yet here I was, upright and conscious. She was unimpressed.

But I was on a high. To be sitting around waiting for the inevitable would have been much harder, emotionally. I was getting a kick out of so much action; and was also lured into a sense that something was being done. I can't stand waiting, or inaction. It makes me very jittery.

The next day, still feeling vaguely superhuman after the port operation, I drove to another city clinic for a heart scan and ECG — some chemo drugs (including epirubicin, which was one of the drugs in my treatment cocktail) can damage the heart, so the docs test for pre-existing heart conditions. It's a very simple procedure: the ECG[42] records the electrical activity of the heart, via little sticky pads (electrodes) placed around your torso, which measure things like the heartbeat rhythm, the size of heart chambers, heart muscle cell damage, etc. The heart scan is an ultrasound[43], adding more information to the picture of your heart function, the most uncomfortable part of the procedure being the cold gel smeared over your chest. I was in and out in about 20 minutes.

By the weekend I was all out of superhuman credits. For daughter's birthday I had organised a special trip for her and five of her wee chums to be taken into Edinburgh to the cinema, and then for a meal.

So let's recap: that week I had undergone a minor operation under local anaesthetic to insert a portacath in my chest; had had vaccinations against both flu and pneumococcal infection; and had driven into hospital to have an (admittedly very quick and easy) ECG and heart scan. By the time daughter's birthday weekend arrived, I was shattered. I successfully commandeered mother-in-law, who graciously agreed to replace me and accompany husband as he shepherded the girls into town. Son also went with them, proud of his given role as mature chaperone.

While they were all gone, I sat in the back garden and drank tea with a friend. That peaceful space was the calm before the storm.

The Appendicitis

The problem with having what seems an all-encompassing illness like cancer is that the rest of real life doesn't stop. There are birthdays and events and other people's illnesses to contend with, littering an already stony path with even more obstacles.

At the time, you march on. You have to. You have to continue with routines and normality, and you do, without much thought. (Though there may be the odd stumbling swear word.) It's only when you look back that you think, how the hell did I cope?

Son couldn't help becoming ill at a crucially emotionally vulnerable period, but that's what happened.

So. It's daughter's seventh birthday party, and husband, mother-in-law and son have accompanied six wee girls into the city for a cinema and burger extravaganza.

On their return, it was noted that son had been feeling a little unwell. He explained that he had a sore stomach. I thought he just needed a poo. Later that evening, he spiked a slight fever, which confounded my poo theory but which failed to concern us too much. On the Monday I was due to go into clinic to have a pre-chemo conversation with one of the nurses; the chemo itself was to start on Wednesday.

Son's slight temperature on the Saturday night had not continued the rest of the weekend; though once he was sick. But he continued to complain about his sore tummy. On Monday morning, he crawled from his bed to the toilet, because it was too painful for him to stand up. The alarm bells which had failed to ring at all began chiming loudly and persistently.

"Where is the pain in your tummy?" I asked son.

"It was here," he said, rubbing a patch below his belly button, "but now it's moved over here," and he patted the right side of his stomach.

Fortunately, husband was working from home that day, and was on school drop-off duty. "Could you make an appointment for son to see the doctor?" I asked him as I rushed out the door for my chemo nurse appointment. "The pain has moved to his side; it could be appendicitis."

Sitting with lovely nurse GH in a small room at the hospital, I was handed various leaflets and slips of paper with information about chemotherapy and all the possible side effects. GH took some blood from my arm, and we sat and chatted. When my phone chirruped its "you have a message" tone, I immediately interrupted the conversation to check it.

"Got an early appointment at doc and they say it's his appendix," read the message from husband. "So going into Sick Kids just now."

"Shit! Okay," I typed back.

But I was strangely emotionless. This was a situation that required calmness and rational thinking. In fact, I don't remember seeing it as "a situation" at all. I finished the meeting with GH, gathered my things and called for a taxi. I breathed in. Out. In. Out. I suspended all maternal feelings and allowed the taxi and the day to carry me where I needed to be.

When I arrived at Sick Kids Hospital (which, as nurse DE later pointed out, was somewhat tautologous – it is surely unnecessary to preface "Kids Hospital" with the word "Sick"), son and husband were sitting in the triage waiting room. And there we stayed for an hour or so, son sitting quietly, patiently and in some degree of discomfort. When, eventually, a nurse called his name, he stood but was in such pain he could only shuffle at an agonisingly slow pace along the corridor. The nurse fetched a wheelchair.

A (newly qualified) junior doctor prodded son's stomach and struggled to take blood (son hadn't drunk anything for a few hours by this point, and his veins had sunk from immediate view). Despite his newfound fear of giving blood[*], son remained still and stoic. The doctor agreed that it was appendicitis and son was admitted to the ward.

He took his place in a bed in a row on the ward; one in a line of pale-faced children, each flanked by parents and sometimes siblings. It seems very strange now, but reflecting on that ward, what comes back to me is

---

[*] A fear initiated by a blood test he had had the year before, which made him so nervous and tense that afterwards, when we left the clinic, he fainted in my arms

the sense of comfort, of safety, of having nothing to worry about. It was the very best place for these children to be – in a calm environment, girded by loved ones and within sight, sound and easy reach of the incredible, kind, capable nurses.

A registrar came to the bed and pressed down on son's stomach. She seemed far more non-committal than the previous medics: "It could be appendicitis but it doesn't seem necessary to operate now. It's not very serious. We'll probably keep him in overnight to keep an eye on him."

Wait until it gets worse? Okay, I thought. Maybe it'll go away. Husband set off on the 40-mile round trip home to pick up son's pyjamas and toothbrush. And while he was gone, the consultant arrived on the ward, made a confident assessment of son's state and said, "Oh yes, it's appendicitis alright. We'll operate on him as soon as possible. Before it gets worse."

"Operate… now?" I asked, a brief skirmish of panic in my stomach at the thought that husband wouldn't be here.

"Yes. Now," said the consultant.

And now, as I type this, I have a sudden sting of tears at the memory of my baby being taken through for an operation. He was so very nervous, but fought to keep from crying, fought to stop his voice skittering up into the frightened high notes as he asked, "What if the anaesthetic doesn't work? Will I feel it go into my arm?"

Those nurses, those anaesthetists… Words cannot express my gratitude for their gentle composure. They had done this so many times they couldn't be blamed for being distant and matter-of-fact – but they weren't. They were soothing and understanding. They worked fast to insert the needle in son's arm.

"What's that? I can feel it. It's cold," he spoke fast. "Is that the anaesthetic now?" The anaesthetists murmured comfortingly, and I stroked his head and told him how much I loved him. And then the nurse said, "That's him gone now. Let's go."

"Gone? I said. "Really?" I held back and worriedly peered at son's closed eyes. That had happened so quickly.

"Yes, he's fast asleep," she said kindly. "You can sit in the ward, and when he's back in the recovery room I'll come and get you."

I had never felt so empty as I did walking away from my baby.

I don't remember how I spent the next hour. Did I read? Surf Twitter?

Watch the nurses at their station busying themselves quietly and efficiently? Yes, all of those, probably. I texted husband. "Son has gone in for surgery xx."

"What? That was a dramatic turnaround of events. What happened?" came the alarmed reply.

"Don't panic – just head doctor decision," I typed back, realising how much emptier than me husband must be feeling, 20 miles away as his nine-year-old son was wheeled in for surgery.

And then the nurse beckoned me through to the recovery room, where son was slowly and dazedly surfacing from anaesthesia. I stroked his face and held back tears of relief.

I thought the hard part was over then, but it wasn't, not really.

Husband stayed overnight with son in hospital, and I spent that night alone at home – daughter had been shipped off to mother-in-law's. I don't recall struggling to sleep – it might seem heartless to be able to fall into a peaceful slumber when neither of one's babies is safe under the same roof as oneself. But I was so tired; tired of having everything taken out of my control. Emotionally exhausted.

The next morning, however, I woke unusually early. At 6.50am I texted husband. "I'll be heading in in about 20 mins – anything you can think of that you need?"

The reply came: "Probably you needn't come so early... I'd wait until after rush hour... son seems fine..."

"I'm coming anyway," I testily texted back. "What else would I do?"

Because what else would I do? I could get caught in the commuter hordes and be sitting in queues but at least I would have the sense of going somewhere, of doing something, of reeling myself back to my boy, on that invisible, imaginary but powerful cord that binds me to my children. I would rather chance the vague irritation of rush hour traffic than wander round the house; worry and an absent mind making me totally incapable of doing anything useful and constructive.

I drove in.

What became harder to deal with than the pain son endured, and the fear as he disappeared from view into the operating theatre, was his sudden depression brought on by enforced rest. Exercise helps boost mood, that's a fact. It's not one I've ever seen tested by my children, who are always active. This was the first time, really, that son was forced to remain lying down for any length of time, and found it too painful even to stand up and make his way to the toilet. He put off visiting the bathroom for as long as possible to avoid the agony of movement.

He became whiny and complaining; when his attempt to colour in a picture of R2-D2 failed to go to plan, he flung the colouring book aside and sobbed with annoyance. There is no reasoning with a nine-year-old in this position. There is no explaining the physical reasons for his mental nosedive, and no comfort in promises that things will get better. Children do not look ahead to see the light at the end of the tunnel – they live solely in the moment.

"You shouldn't really be visiting the hospital," said a friend when I saw her later that day. "You're about to start chemo so your immune system will be compromised very soon." But I felt fine. Like my son, I was living in the moment – and at that moment, he needed me.

The next day, Wednesday, was my first chemotherapy session. Mum came with me to sit with son, having travelled up from the south of England to stay and help out for a few days. Son watched *Dr Who* on iPlayer. He ate an apple. His mood was the lowest I have ever known it. When husband arrived to take me to the chemo clinic, son started crying. Mum was staying with him, and I knew he would be fine, but my god, having to walk away from your child when every ounce of his little being, from his face to his tears to his broken words, is imploring you to stay is heartbreaking. I smiled and kissed him and hugged him and walked away.

Once through the door, I cracked and sobbed.

While we were gone, the consultant, on his ward round, expressed his satisfaction with son's recovery. "Where are his mum and dad?" he asked.

"His mum is having her first chemo session right now," said mum.

"Oh, well he won't be going home tonight then," said the consultant.

Son did come home the next day, though, and made himself

comfortable in the lounge, which we turned into a hospital ward. The sofa bed was opened up, and he shuffled between that and the downstairs loo. Once home, his mood immediately lifted; his recovery was so fast, I marvelled at the strength and fitness of young bodies. His tenth birthday, on the Saturday, saw him propped upright on the couch, covered in a warm blanket, handed gift after gift. His smile as he opened each Lego box was all the reassurance I needed that he was going to be just fine.

Chapter Eight

The first day of chemo. I dragged myself away from my crying boy, leaving him in the more than capable hands of mum. And the nurses, of course. I pulled myself together on the car journey to the other hospital, breathing deeply and telling myself that everything would be okay. It would have to be.

I am fascinated by the brain's capabilities, its strengths, weaknesses, peccadilloes, channels of reasoning, habits and foibles. If I were any cleverer or could be arsed, I'd like to study psychology and the emotional impact of trauma on the human brain. (I'd also like to write novels, excel as an investigative journalist, own an eco house in Shetland and an apartment in Cadiz, run a bookshop, and help children with dyslexia form a constructive and positive relationship with books and reading, so don't set too much store by my ambitions.)

That first day in the chemo chair was not so much a rollercoaster of emotions as a whirlwind, log flume, bungee jump, skydive, mountain climb and 3D cinematic experience all-rolled-into-one of emotions.

Despite the deep breathing in the car, when I sat in that chemo chair my heart beat was insistently fast, my blood pressure throat-constrictingly high. The muscles in my neck and shoulders were so tense I thought they'd crack. I was faintly hysterical, a fake grin smeared on my face, an attempt at jollity masking the panic within. Suppress the fear. Don't admit to weakness. Stay positive. Giving in to anxiety will only make this harder.

I was fitted with the cold cap[44], a contrivance that is intended to reduce the likelihood of hair loss, though it works in roughly only 25% of cases. It's a deeply uncomfortable contraption, through which ice cold gel is pumped — it's like having brain freeze for the first 15 minutes it's on. But I have very thick hair, so it wasn't so much the extreme cold that got me as the tightness; in order for the cold cap to work, it needs to fit as snugly as possible round your scalp. This meant having the strap pulled tight beneath my chin, which scrunched up my cheeks and made me look like a helmeted hamster. Or a 50s sci-fi cartoon.

Cold cap in place, nurse GH began unpacking the needles and tubes she would be attaching to the port in my chest. The port. I still wasn't used to the port. It was an overt, alien lump in my chest; whenever I ran my fingers over it my stomach rolled with nausea. Husband had applied the local anaesthetic cream at home — a small tube of the stuff which went on an hour before the appointment, so that the needle plunging in would not be felt.

But here was GH about to plunge in that needle. My breathing sped up, I could actually feel a release of adrenaline, I wanted to fidget, I wanted to run, I couldn't breathe, the edges of my vision went blurry and unclear…

"It's okay," I smiled, "I'm just having an anxiety attack." When I first began having anxiety attacks, some years ago, the onset of these symptoms would have terrified me as much as whatever set off the anxiety attack in the first place. These days I get a perverse sense of control knowing that that is all they are — symptoms. Symptoms of something basically harmless. They are supremely unpleasant but they will pass. Husband said nothing but rifled through my handbag and handed me a tab of diazepam.

Diazepam. That drug again. Do you think I was too heavily reliant on the stuff? I'll let you into a little secret: it's the only thing that works for me.

Some people talk of mindfulness. Of meditation. Of yoga and gongs and deep breathing. I tried yoga once. It made me fart and feel sick. Gongs would irritate me. Deep breathing sometimes helps, if I can pre-empt the panic attack — it's rarely useful halfway through. I don't even know what mindfulness[45] is, apart from the latest buzz word. Horses for courses, and all that — diazepam works. Oh, right, the stigma of anti-anxiety drugs. Well, that's a load of rubbish, isn't it? They're prescription, they're not poison. They work. They're proven to work. If you have a broken leg, you use a crutch. If you have a broken arm you put it in a sling. If you have a headache you drink more water, have a poo, and then take paracetamol. If you struggle to control your fears and anxiety in a stressful situation, you pop a diazepam. Frankly, I wish I'd discovered it years before I did.

It would have saved a lot of grief and paved the way to a much more laidback lifestyle.

Here endeth the lesson.

The painful image of my crying boy's face, which hung in my mind like a gothic curtain, gradually faded with the onset of the drug's power. My fear of the needle that GH was soon to insert dissipated. I sat back, breathed deeply again. GH gently forced the needle into my port, a pinching sensation deep inside making me yelp. "It's just because you still have bruising from the operation," said GH. "You won't feel it next time."

And then a sequence of drugs began coursing through my veins. I was pumped with supportive drugs such as antiemetics and steroids, followed by the chemo — epirubicin and cyclophosphamide — which was a garish, gruesome blood red.

I sat back and prepared to do nothing for two hours.

Husband and I passed some time composing poems on our mobile phones, which caused some fairly hysterical hilarity. I'm pretty sure the other patients would have wondered why we thought the chemo process was so funny. To be honest, the poems weren't that amusing, but the anxiety and fear that had been swamping me left me teetering on the edge of a river of nervous energy, and the unwarranted laughter released a complex mix of emotions.

Using predictive text, husband's best offering went:

> *Could you please email me the peacock*
> *Thanks for your email and any attachments*
> *I will be in the office today*
> *I will be in the office today*
> *I will be in the office today.*

My own creations resulted in this pearl of wisdom:

> *The next day is a good idea*
> *It's not like you have to do something*
> *The next time you have to come*
> *I would like a good book.*

A demand I stand by.

Try it — it's a genre I'm calling predictive poetry.

After two hours of sitting in the cold cap, I was released from the chair and husband drove me home, returning to Sick Kids to sit with son and allow mum to come home to me. I curled up in bed and waited for the impact of the cytotoxins. Though I had been given antiemetics and the chemo nurses did not expect me to be sick, for the next few hours I lay surfing a rising and falling nausea, accompanied by stomach cramps and a general sensation of severe discomfort. I would sleep, then wake feeling uncomfortable and sick, then the nausea would ebb away and I slept again.

Amidst the queasiness, mother-in-law returned with daughter, who had been staying with her for the past three nights. I had missed her cheeky little face, big blue eyes and reassuring detachment from all the tribulations, and desperately wanted to hug her but had only enough energy to take her hand and give her a smile. Even this was too much — my body revolted against such a movement and I threw up bile into a bowl.

The day after chemo, it was necessary to drop into the local cottage hospital to have a pegfilgrastim injection, the syringe and drug having been provided by my chemo clinic. Pegfilgrastim[46] is a PEGylated form of the recombinant human granulocyte colony-stimulating factor analog filgrastim. Snort. That's what it says on Wikipedia. Basically, chemo attacks and kills white blood cells — neutrophils — as well as the cancer cells. The white blood cells fight infection, so obviously you are vulnerable to infection just after a blast of chemo. Pegfilgrastim stimulates the body's production of neutrophils so your immune system gets up to speed again.

I wobbled to the hospital and presented a nurse with the syringe. It seemed to be some sort of fancy application system because she struggled to work it out and put it together, but then kindly managed to apply it and send me on my way, back home to bed. (Thank Bevan for the NHS. It must be saved.)

For four days it was as though I had been through a wringer, an ultra marathon or bodily pummelling. I slept almost constantly, waking only to take antiemetics and eat. And boy, thanks to the steroids did I have an appetite. I was sent back to memories of my pregnancies, which both involved a lot of sickness, and almost perpetual cream cracker-consumption to stave off the nausea.

I did manage to get out of bed and descend the stairs two days after the pegfilgrastim jab to watch son, snuggled under blankets and propped up on cushions, open his birthday presents. He was unhappy at missing out on the go-karting with mates we had planned, but was suitably cheered by the stacks of Lego. It wasn't quite the tenth birthday celebration he might have wished for, but it would certainly be memorable.

After a couple of days, the nausea passed and a degree of energy returned, though only enough to walk slowly to the nearby park for some fresh air. I was dressed and I was out. Showering could wait. (This also took me back to second pregnancy, when I was so sick I couldn't sit up without throwing up, and consequently didn't wash for six weeks. Yup. I stank, obvs.)

But I was determined to cut myself some slack. I was often presented with stories of other cancer patients who managed to get to the gym, run marathons, "fight" and "battle" their illness. I felt inadequate in the face of such superhumans, of course. I wondered at their strength and energy. I reasoned that they must be on different drugs (and there are a lot of chemo drugs, of differing strength and impact). I did feel inferior. I was weaker, less positive. But I also listened to my body. If I was weaker, I would rest. If I was less positive, I would hold my children tight, smile at them, love them more than my heart could bear.

One week after the chemo session, I was back at the clinic for blood tests. The white blood cell levels had to be measured. I sat in the chair, and it was only after a minute or so of nurse KL preparing the needles that I realised she intended to take blood from the port in my chest. The realisation thrust me rapidly into a small moment of panic. "Oh no," I said, "Can you do it from my arm?" The portacath system is by far the best way to insert and remove fluids over a period of time. It saves on scarring of the veins. It's highly functional and effective. But I hated it. I hated that alien lump. I could tolerate having the chemo mobilised in this way, because it was necessary, but I was damned if I would have blood removed from it too, when I had a perfectly acceptable arm. For some strange (possibly traditional) reason, I was perfectly okay with the idea of having a needle inserted in the crook of my elbow. But I didn't want any more attention paid to that port thing than was necessary. I hadn't taken any diazepam. I would need diazepam before anyone even thought of approaching my port.

KL disposed of the port needles, and came back with a good old-fashioned hypodermic. The blood was taken from my arm.

"Nine out of ten patients need antibiotics after their first chemo cycle," said GH, explaining the necessity for testing neulasta levels. Those nasty cytotoxins destroy white blood cells and platelets, and this attack on the body's immune system can come as something of a shock. You need a boost, a kick start to white cell production, hence the pegfilgrastim then a follow-up blood test and, in all likelihood, a blast of antibiotics.

"You can go home now," said GH. "We'll call you later this afternoon when we have the result and probably issue an antibiotic prescription."

But when they did call me, it was to say that though my white blood cell count was naturally lower than normal, Dr B did not believe it warranted antibiotics. Ha — apparently I was a fighter. I was the one out of ten who didn't need the support of antibiotics.

And then a few days later my throat swelled up dramatically, red and sore. Husband shone a torch in my mouth, looking for white patches — signs of oral thrush. Mmmm, lovely. One of the many side effects of chemo to be expected. There were no white patches to be seen but, as instructed, I called the chemo nurses to let them know about the swelling. "Okay, well just make sure husband keeps an eye on it," said GH, "and in the meantime, gargle twice a day with antiseptic mouthwash. And don't worry."

It's actually very hard not to worry, when after the very first chemo session one is beset by a minor virus, despite being a one-in-ten warrior. Which of the many other predicted side-effects would fell me and when? The important thing to do in this situation is not stay in bed, wrapped up in a cotton duvet, allowing no-one in to see you, especially not your children, who are generally the ones guilty of bringing all manner of disgusting viruses and illnesses home from school, caught from their unsavoury peers. To shut yourself away would be to give in.

Besides which, brother and his family were due to visit a few days later, and I was damned if I would call a halt to their plans. I rarely see my niece and nephew, and I love them with that affection that one feels for flesh and blood. Well, you know, only if they're decent people. It's hard to love a twat, no matter how closely related they are. But niece and nephew are children, so they haven't had the opportunity to develop any twatty characteristics yet.

Just before they arrived, however, brother texted me.

"Forgot to say earlier, but S has got a little sniffle at the moment. Wasn't sure if that would be a problem with your reduced immune system?"

"I'm not supposed to be in enclosed spaces like trains with lots of humans and potential illnesses," I replied. But was there any point in keeping a sniffly niece away when I had my own two germ-magnets? "With two kids at school I can't be too precious about it. Don't cancel the train just yet."

"S seems to constantly have a snotty nose so it's sometimes difficult to know whether she really has got a cold. We could maybe keep her in the garden?"

"It's okay... Just as long as I don't lick her face it'll be fine."

And then snotty niece, mischievous nephew, brother and sister-in-law were with us, and all thoughts of illnesses, side effects, nausea and blood cell count were banished by the general mayhem and hilarity. It's pretty impossible to remain introspective and self-obsessed when there's a small child under your feet constantly asking "why?"

"I shouldn't give the cat her meat because she hasn't finished her breakfast biscuits," I said one afternoon, as niece looked on curiously.

"Why?" asked niece.

"She probably wasn't hungry."

"Why?" At this point I realised I'd been had, and this conversation could potentially go on for some time. I resolved to answer every single "Why" and never give in.

"Maybe she caught mice in the field last night and ate those."

"Why?"

"Because she was hungry...?" Niece mulled this over and was either satisfied by the answer or herself realised this could be a circular and never-ending conversation. She remained silent. *I win*, I thought with immature smugness.

And nephew was a hoot, his natural caution and trepidation cast aside, thanks to a year in primary school, which had varnished his sensitivity with a brash coating of machismo. "Pshhhhhhh, pshhhhhhh!" he hissed as he pretended to squirt boiling hot lava from a rubberised toy slug into my face at every opportunity.

"Oh dear," I said, spooning cereal into my mouth.

"Your face is melting and your eyeballs will fall out," said nephew with relish. This new direction in his personality did make me wonder what sort of little toerags he's been hanging out with, because nephew is a lovely wee soul.

It was this very familiar, cosy reality that kept me from dropping into absolute indifference. The neediness of children, their naivety and direct line to reality. There's nothing disingenuous about children. Even when they think they're mimicking the grown-ups and engaging in some sort of mild deception, they are so transparent, so easily foiled and quick to be sorry. Their blunt curiosity. Their lack of agenda. Their absolute subconscious insistence that you stop obsessing about yourself and pay them attention. Small children are the very best mental health medicine.

And after the second chemo session, my hair began to fall out.

I swept a hand through my thick, coarse tresses and clumps came out in my balled fist. It was a weird sensation — I felt both resigned and perplexed at the same time. Despite knowing hair loss could be one of the side effects, when it actually happened it was a shock. In the shower, entire locks were sluiced down my body and into the plug hole. My stomach turned and I couldn't look. So much for the cold cap, then.

And fairly soon after that came a string of other side effects, so predictable I felt belittled. I was not special. I wasn't the first to have breast cancer and wouldn't be the last. My suffering was so common, the doctors knew exactly what would happen to me. This should have been reassuring but it was nevertheless a surprise.

My body began to succumb to the chemo in such a way I was disgusted by its weakness. Husband reminded me that all these signs of "weakness" were proof that the chemo was working. But I felt my body had betrayed me. It turned out I wasn't so special or different after all. I wasn't kooky or unpredictable or tough or out-of-the-ordinary. I was entirely normal. Absolutely vulnerable. My gums began bleeding; oral thrush set in; and constipation was a given.

The Prunes

Much of my life has been spent in a state of constipation. This is almost certainly my fault. I don't eat enough fruit and vegetables for a start. Also – and I think this is the greater reason – all stress and anxiety goes straight to my digestive system. I am a firm believer in psychosomatic illness (probably because I'm convinced I suffer it). In my early 20s I was diagnosed with irritable bowel syndrome – that great catch-all which is used to explain any number of symptoms which don't quite add up to a curable disease. In my mid-20s, as mentioned before, following my near-death accident I went through a period of suddenly vomiting in the middle of the night.

But any and all these odd symptoms were fleeting, in comparison with the decades of poolessness I have endured. This started at university, and was almost certainly in response to my suddenly terrible, fruit-free diet. Uni friends fed me coffee, claiming it would loosen me up. It didn't. The only thing that got my bowels moving in those wanton, nutrition-free days was a violent hangover. And since that was due to my poor body attempting to rid itself of noxious toxins, those waste discharges were hardly healthy.

Five years later, living and working in London, I mentioned my concrete craps on the phone to mum. Being so bunged up has a horribly detrimental effect on one's health and wellbeing. It made me sluggish, bloated and usually nauseated.

"Prunes!" said mum. "You just need to eat some prunes. That'll sort you out."

I bought a packet of prunes.

At that time I was working as a freelance sub-editor. I had been invited by the editor of a title I had recently worked on to go to hers for dinner. It would be informal, but I didn't know her particularly well, and had never met her partner.

That afternoon, with nothing better to do, I sat on my bed in the cold London flat I shared with two other young women, read a book and ate the prunes. All 20 of them.

Shortly after I had finished the packet, my stomach set up an orchestra of the most astonishing noises: gurgling and bubbling in such a way I felt as though there was an eddying stream wending its way around my gut. I listened to the alien sounds, fascinated and a little worried. I wondered whether I should go out for dinner that night after all. But though my stomach burbled and churned away, I didn't actually feel unwell. So off I went.

I'm sure the evening would have been very pleasant if it wasn't for the fact that my bowels exploded. Sitting at the dinner table, I could barely concentrate on whatever conversation there was, so perturbed was I by the dancing in my midriff. Very suddenly, I realised what the intestinal turmoil had been leading to, and I rushed to the bathroom.

I had to rush to the bathroom about five times before I thought it would be safe enough for me to get a taxi the shortish journey home. Each visit to the bathroom was concluded with my spraying quantities of room freshener, whose chemical perfume pervaded the flat and betrayed my troublesome bowels.

I never saw my host again.

"You're only supposed to have two or three prunes a day," said mum.

Chapter Nine

All the minor side effects of chemo were bearable, if irritating. That is, bleeding gums could be protected by regular mouthwashes. Oral thrush was prescribed an aniseed-flavoured medicine to clear it. As for the constipation… though cheats such as Fybogel were recommended, I preferred to turn to those good old-fashioned natural remedies such as prunes and pineapple.

The hair loss was devastating, to begin with. It was nauseating. To avoid looking patchy and diseased, I instructed husband to shave it all off, which he did with relish. As I sat on the chair in the kitchen, covered in towels, I held my breath – not because I was sorry to be losing my thick locks but because I was terrified the electric clippers would slice into my head. Of course they didn't. They don't work like that.

When they buzzed next to my ears it was as much as I could do not to scream. I pictured all the amazingly striking women I knew who had shaved their heads – Ripley, Sinead O'Connor, Jessie J… Of course, I wouldn't look like them. I had none of their beauty. When I had my hair cut short for the first time ever, in the final year of primary school, some boy laughed at my ears and said I looked like ET's mum. I still have the ears, so I figured I'd still look misshapen without any hair.

But I honestly wasn't that bothered once it was all off. Rather a shaved head than have clumps of hair come out in my hands. I've had my hair long and short throughout my life – I was used to different styles. Having it shaved didn't come as a shock – not then, anyway. Since then, when I have looked back at photos, I say, "My God, did I look like that? I don't remember looking like that. I had no hair!"

But the children, whose reaction to a bald mum I worried about, seemed unfazed. They said nothing. They still hugged me and climbed into bed with us in the mornings. I didn't disgust them, and that was a relief. And though husband's cautious grade 2 cut left me with noticeably balder patches, even these disappeared as the remaining stubble fell out. I no longer looked diseased so much as properly ill.

What I hadn't appreciated about the hair loss was that it would affect my entire body. Well, apart from my big toes, which managed to remain somewhat hirsute probably by virtue of being all the way down there at the bottom of my body, furthest away from the chemo entry site.

The first hair I lost was in the groin area, which was a joy, if I'm honest. As a very dark-haired woman, maintenance of that area has been nothing but a pain in the arse. Oh! Not literally. As I resembled more and more a Barbie doll, I almost felt sexy. Not that Barbie dolls... oh never mind.

Also the armpits, which became beautifully smooth and utterly kempt[*]. What did take me aback was the impact of having no nasal hair. Ah yes – one also loses one's nasal hair. And if you thought nasal hair had no biological part to play, you're sadly wrong – I discovered that it holds back the tidal waves of snot. Having lost this barrier, any streams of mucus would simply fall, without warning and unchecked, straight out my nose. That was pretty hideous.

The second worst impact[**] of chemo was the exhaustion. It wasn't even a real, physical tiredness – it was something more akin to a hangover: the body had been poisoned, and so the brain put it to sleep while it mended and recovered. Four or five days would pass after each session of eprirubicin and cyclophosphamide in a cloudy fug. And then I would rise, like a phoenix from the ashes, renewed and breathing deeply, as the cytotoxins were cleared from my system. This rising was always so blissful; such a glorious sensation, after the semi-conscious and sweating state of just post-chemo. That said, even in this risen state, sitting upright for any length of time was a challenge, as was talking in extended sentences, which left me breathless with the exertion.

The surfacing from my second session coincided beautifully with the General Election. I say beautifully; I was delighted to be able to get out of bed and go and vote – something I might not have been able to do if

[*] I'm assuming something can be kempt, if it isn't unkempt?
[**] You'll get to the first worst in a minute

election day had been straight after chemo. I love a General Election. The blood of the suffragettes rampages through my veins, and to miss a vote, or even the political debate on social media, would have been unthinkable.

But the General Election was one of the very few occasions I managed to engage in. Many other planned events fell by the wayside of my sick bed.

Apparently, there are some freakish individuals who can power through the nausea, exhaustion and weakness, and continue living an almost normal life. I say freakish individuals, obviously I mean brave heroes. One woman who sat in the chemo chair next to mine announced that she was still going into work between sessions. I marvelled at her energy and dedication. Well, I marvelled after I had revelled in the guilt I felt at being much more useless than she was. On one occasion, when picking up daughter from school, I suddenly felt so feeble that I had to offload her to one friend, while another gave me a lift home. I always had the intention of living normally, but sometimes my body simply let me down. Wouldn't co-operate.

Which meant that I had to take a deckchair to son and daughter's school sports day; where all the other parents were expected to stand and watch, I moved my deckchair around the events and sat with regal pomp. For some reason, rather than avoid drawing attention to myself, I decided to wear a turquoise wig that day, which very much attracted attention to me and my deckchair. It's almost as though I was trying to emphasise how special I was.

At least I made it to sports day. Other events – such as a work PR event; a wine-related night out with mums; son's rock school gig; the local summer raft race; and an end-of-term beach party (which had been optimistically noted in my diary) – passed by unattended by me.

The first worst side effect of chemo was the breakdown of my sense of taste. I have no idea why chemo should have such an impact on one's tastebuds…. Hang on, I'll look it up…

Oh great. Apparently it's unclear, but the best guess is that chemo, in its terrorising of all things living, also damages cells, including taste buds, in the oral cavity.

Well, I could have told you that.

What happened was that everything tasted of either lardy past-its-use-by-date yoghurt or metal, and often both. I'd never really considered myself a foodie, but bloody hell did I miss the simple flavours of grub. Husband served every dish with the proud query, "What do you think?" and I would answer, "It tastes like shit. Everything tastes like shit." This was nothing to do with husband's culinary efforts, as he's a pretty good cook when he can be arsed, and everything to do with the fact that fatty food such as chips coated the roof of my mouth in lard, and olives were mere balls of iron ore on my disillusioned tongue.

Food became nothing but a chore, fuel that I wolfed down out of necessity, and without any enjoyment.

The night before round two of chemo, when, theoretically, I should have been feeling at the height of my energy levels, I was actually tired and emotional, which made going out for dinner, as we did, perhaps the wrong decision. Daughter's own anxieties surfaced in a sore tummy – or, at least, the claim to be having one – which made me think that, like brother, she might be coming down with appendicitis just in time for my next chemotherapy session. I was sweary and full of self-pity, and not quick enough to realise that daughter herself just wanted cuddles and reassurance.

And, of course, she wasn't unwell, so managed to go to school the next day, which allowed me to get to hospital for my second course of chemo. I was tense with trepidation as GH approached me with the needle, remembering the bruised pain as she inserted it into my newly acquired port two weeks previously.

But her assurances that the swelling would have reduced were correct (of course they were!), and I felt almost nothing as she slid the needle smoothly through my skin into the port beneath.

I answered a series of questions about how I had been after the first chemo session – I told them I had felt very sick, and this time I was prescribed five – count 'em – anti-emetics. "I challenge you to feel sick this time," said DE.

Not that I didn't trust her, but when husband had driven me home, I curled up in bed and awaited the nausea-surfing. It didn't come. There were no cramps and no real sickness – just a faint queasiness that was dispelled by constant eating…

I slept, though. Slept for a few days. And when I woke I stuffed my face with fruit salad, prunes, potato waffles, Weetabix and pineapple. Before I was ill, I associated cancer patients with paleness, scrawniness, weakness. But, to be brutally honest, that properly ill aesthetic is reserved for the cancer patients who are coming to the end of their journey; they cannot eat. But when your prognosis is good, you look bizarrely healthy, thanks to the steroids that are included in the chemo mix. I do remember being told about the steroids, but I don't remember realising what imbibing them would mean. It meant I was constantly peckish.

I stuffed my face. And I put on weight. My cheeks were rounded and rosy, though pairing this increasing roundedness with my increasing baldness did make me feel like Humpty Dumpty. "You look really well!" people would say with surprise when they saw me, obviously assuming, like I did before I knew all this, that I should be looking bloody ghastly. It's very hard to persuade people you're ill when your face is glowing. It's very hard for them to believe that you feel slightly sick and very tired, when your cheeks are a vibrantly healthy hue. It's very difficult for friends and family to picture the cancer cells attempting to eat you from the inside out, when you are piling on the pounds.

So. Just to say that even if a person looks well, doesn't mean they are.

I especially didn't feel very well after the second cycle of chemo, when I took something of an over-exuberant approach to dispelling the constipation that had set in. Having apparently learned nothing from that embarrassing episode in London, I downed not just prunes but also Fybogel and pineapple, the last of which a dietician friend had recommended as a constipation cure. Needless to say, shortly after that my guts exploded, for a full two days. That's two days of expelling every last ounce of food and nutrition from my body, with absolutely no respite. I was exhausted. I was actually terrified. I seemed to have opened the floodgates of hell, and I was being drained to death. I cried with self-pity.

"Maybe don't take all three of them," said GH when I turned up for the blood test a day later. By that time I had recovered somewhat, and was able to laugh at myself.

And then, after chemo cycle 2's blood test, I was told that my liver function results were abnormal; that is, abnormal even by chemo standards. I would need an ultrasound to make sure my liver hadn't finally caved under the pressure of all those toxins. I was slightly concerned;

I thought perhaps years of drinking too much alcohol might have compromised my liver's stamina (though I didn't say as much). The nurse ran through a number of acronyms, none of which meant anything to me: ALPs, ALTs, ASTs and LDHs. All of them were up, apparently; I just nodded, and waited to be told what to do.

Ultrasound, then. Off I dutifully went, to have the cold gel smeared over my midriff, and the sensor rolled across my body. A call from GH later that day, after I had returned home, gave me the all clear. "There's no scarring, and no damage," she said. "We think the dip in your liver performance is because of the medication you had for the oral thrush." So my liver would bounce back to its normal fully functional self, now I had finished the oral thrush treatment. I just had to hope oral thrush wouldn't return.

These side effects were really quite tiresome.

The Relocation

What kept me going? Sheer bloodymindedness. Faith in medicine. A disbelief I could die, let alone would. And above all, above everything, husband. My kind, patient, pragmatic husband.

I fell in love with husband as soon as I saw him across the crowded pub. How I hadn't seen him before this fateful night I've no idea, since we were both at a mutual friend's birthday party, and we had both been to the same friend's birthday parties on at least two previous years. And yet there we were – oblivious of one another's existence until November 2004.

Anyway, I was sitting at a table in a Tooting pub, chatting to a mate, when I looked up and saw this regal chap, heads above those around him, straight back, aquiline nose… "Who is that?" I asked in a suggestive tone of voice. Nobody at my table knew. So I made it my business to find out.

To cut another long story short, I was introduced to him but

> 1) he was with a girl
> 2) the music was so loud I couldn't hear a word he said
> 3) after several years of forcing my fingers into romantic fires and having them burnt, I had sworn off chasing men.

The evening ended with us failing to exchange contact details.

"What did you think of husband*?" asked our mutual friend when I saw her next. "You spoke to him, didn't you?"

"Yes, he seemed nice enough," I said cagily.

"He and his girlfriend aren't really getting on at the moment," she said,

---

* She didn't call him that! That's silly. But that's his name in this book, so…

her agenda so clear she might as well have chiselled it on a plaque and nailed it to my forehead.

"I didn't really speak to her," I said.

"Oh that wasn't his girlfriend! She was just a mate of his he knows through work."

I'd be lying if I said this news didn't send a glimmer of hope into my love-hungry heart. But he still had a girlfriend, and it was nothing to do with me how well they were getting on. I changed the subject.

Four months* later I received an email at work, with words to this effect:

"Hello. I don't know if you remember me. I met you at that birthday party in Tooting. I was the man from Shetland. I wonder if you would like to meet up for a drink."

I turned to the office secretary, held my arms aloft, and said, "I've pulled!"

Turns out, he had managed to hear me over the bloody awful pub music when I'd told him which magazine I worked on; he had gone into the newsagent, picked up the mag and looked through the contacts section to get my email address. How romantic is that?! He didn't buy the magazine, though. Just put it back on the shelf**.

Here's an amazing fact about husband, one that, when I learnt it, impressed me hugely and then, when I was diagnosed with cancer, made me smile at the irony.

Husband did a PhD at Nottingham University, sponsored by Cancer Research Campaign (which later merged with Imperial Cancer Research Fund to become Cancer Research UK). He was based in the pharma sciences department, in the cancer research lab. Yes, he was part of a team working to find cures for cancer. I know, right?

Indeed, a derivative of one he worked on went on to become licensed. If

---

* Four months! Four!

** I just asked husband why he hadn't asked our mutual friend for my contact details, rather than riffle through a magazine in a newsagent's. He said, "You're asking me that now? Erm… I don't know. Because I'm private? To avoid gossip? Because I didn't think of it."

you were paranoid, you'd almost think cancer was getting its own back by attacking his wife. You'd have to be very paranoid.

Anyway, I'm getting to the relocation bit, bear with me. Husband and I were together for about a year before we started talking about moving in together and having children. (We were both about 32, don't panic. Plenty old enough to make grown-up decisions like that. Plus, my biological clock was ticking so loudly it had given me impaired hearing; more to the point, husband didn't seem scared shitless by the ticking.)

We agreed to move to Scotland.

This wasn't as far out a crazy decision as you might think. Husband had just finished an MBA, so was going to strike out on his own, employment-wise. He said he could do his job anywhere. His parents had relocated from Shetland to a wee settlement just east of Edinburgh, so we wouldn't be without supportive contacts north of the border.

I, on the other hand, have always, cheesily or otherwise, identified strongly with my Scottish heritage. My dad's from just north of Glasgow. Much of his family is still in the area. Just before I met husband I had already been planning to move out of London, destroyed as I had been by the city's relentless pace; one of my intended relocations was to Glasgow (I genuinely thought it would be quieter). When husband suggested moving to Scotland, it seemed the natural progression.

He owned a flat on Edinburgh's Royal Mile, where he had lived while a student and which he now rented out each summer to Festival performers. We would make this flat our home, and I would look for work in journalism or publishing.

Ha ha ha ha ha ha ha ha!

Sorry, just getting a bit ahead of myself.

I started redecorating the flat in my head; drawing up plans using my piss-poor InDesign skills. I researched magazines and publishing companies. And at around this time, as we confirmed plans to move, I suggested we give up using contraceptives, because "I didn't know how long it would take to fall pregnant. We better start trying now!"

Ha ha ha ha ha ha ha ha!

I have a best friend who I have known since I was three, when we went to the same playschool. Through the years, we have drifted apart, come together again, met up sporadically, met up frequently… She is always in the orbit of my life though. When we both lived in London, we would meet up for curry and Champagne.

One Saturday, we met in Covent Garden, wandered the shops, then settled down in a bar. "I was due on my period a couple of days ago," I said to her. "It's a bit late and I'm not wearing a pad or anything – can you let me know if I leak*?"

Yes – I wasn't worried about the tardiness of my period, I was worried about the potential for aesthetic humiliation.

Anyway, several hours and a couple of bottles of Champagne later, best mate popped me in a cab to husband's sister's flat, where husband and I were staying the night. I arrived giggling and incomprehensible. Husband put me to bed.

The next morning, I woke with the obligatory hangover. My hangovers are pretty legendary, and usually involve me lying in a dehydrated, headachy stupor until late afternoon.

"I was due on my period a couple of days ago," I mumbled. "It still hasn't arrived."

Husband went and sat at the computer at the end of the bed and started Googling. And then, while I contemplated throwing up, or going back to sleep, or managing my way across the hall to the bathroom, he regaled me with the negative impacts alcohol can have on an unborn baby.

"Foetal Alcohol Syndrome affects the way a baby's brain develops… Drinking alcohol, especially in the first three months of pregnancy, increases the risk of miscarriage, premature birth and your baby having a low birth weight. Foetal Alcohol Spectrum Disorder is associated with a mother's drinking…"

I felt terrible, obviously. Husband had chosen me to propagate his amazing genes and I just wasn't taking it seriously.

I arrived home at seven o'clock that evening, sweaty and tired. I took the pregnancy test (kept in the bathroom cabinet, since we were, after all, trying for a baby), and peed on the stick. It took about 10 seconds for the stick to say "Pregnant".

"Shit," I said out loud. "What have I done?" and a terrified nausea

---

* Too much information? Come on, it's a perfectly normal bodily function

engulfed me. I texted husband, "I'm pregnant!", with a photo of the stick. He texted back a photo which is now lost in the ether, but which I will always remember – a selfie of him grinning like a goon, his thumbs up an enormous icon of happiness in the foreground.

On week six of my pregnancy, the sickness and nausea started. It began as just a constant feeling of queasiness, which I staunched in the office with packets of cream crackers. But it soon developed into actual vomiting every morning, and a basic inability to move without throwing up. I spent the last three weeks of my one-month notice to quit my job lying on my parents' sofa (I had moved out of my flat to make way for a tenant. While husband and brother packed up my things and loaded them into a van, I lay on the bathroom floor, periodically barfing).

But while this immobility prevented me from going to work, it did not stop me heading off on a 10-hour drive to Scotland (it's an eight-hour drive with additional pregnant-woman pee stops). Oh yes! We went ahead and moved! We had to. I had resigned my job. Organised the rental of my flat. It was all a done deal. Oh – ah – but we weren't going to stay in the Royal Mile flat after all. I had decided that the spiral flights of stone stairs up to the second floor would not be suitable for a pregnant woman, or a baby in a pram, or even a toddler in a buggy. So we were going to stay in a rental cottage in the middle of nowhere*, while we looked for a family home to buy.

My memories of this move, and of the start of our lives together, are such a mess of imagery in my mind, I find it difficult to untangle. I look back now and wonder how on earth I managed such a massive change in lifestyle. I had gone from being a pretty carefree working woman in the capital, going out on the lash with my work colleagues, meeting up with old friends from school, university and my journalism course… to being pregnant, jobless, friendless, living for the first time with a partner, in a different country, in the middle of nowhere.

But at the time I took it all in my stride.

The doctor prescribed me some anti-sickness pills for the mammoth

---

* "In the middle of nowhere" is the crucial phrase here. I had been raised in a very big town, then spent the past eight years living and working in London

car journey, and off we went. I spent the next couple of months throwing up every morning, then, in the afternoon when the nausea wore off, going for solo walks around the countryside. I don't remember feeling lonely (although, I did just ask husband where he went to work in those first couple of months in the cottage, and he said, "at the kitchen table." I have absolutely no recollection of husband in that cottage.) I don't remember ever feeling I had made the wrong decision. We went house-hunting, though husband often had to do this alone, since I was prostrate and queasy for much of the time. We intended to travel near and far throughout Scotland, exploring and identifying a location in which to put down roots. But I couldn't be arsed. I was too tired and fed up. We drove through the town nearest to our rural abode and I said, "Can we just live here?" "Well done," said husband. "You've just chosen the most expensive town in Scotland."

We bought a house. The previous owner had been a chain smoker so, you know, it needed all its carpets ripped up, curtains pulled down, windows left open day and night for weeks and all the walls repainted. Also a new kitchen. We stayed in the cottage for the two months it took to complete all this cosmetic stuff. And for those two months, husband got a temporary contract working in London…

So. I'm pregnant. I know nobody. I live in the middle of nowhere. Husband disappears four days of every week. And though the pregnancy sickness has abated, this is replaced by constant urinary tract infections, which get so bad at one point I am sent to hospital overnight for observation and kidney scans. I am alone in a cottage in the countryside, where a moonless night is so black, the darkness is almost tangible, almost chewable. The hooting owls are my companions. The restless, rustling hordes of mice not so much.

And yet… I survived. Well, of course I did, it wasn't a bloody gulag. I went to ante-natal classes, met other soon-to-be mums, joined aquanatal group, had (decaffeinated) coffees and (very sugary) cakes with new friends…

When husband and I finally moved into our newly decorated house, two months before I gave birth, mother-in-law greeted me anxiously at the front door, saying, "Oh, you can't move in now. The boxes aren't unpacked!" She was just looking out for me, eager to have the home nest-ready and spick and span for pregnant me. But I burst into tears and replied, "This is my home. I'm not staying one more night in that cottage." She let me in.

I did survive. I lived through it. I was excited and overwhelmed in equal measure by this so very different chapter of my life. And when I look back, I think, *how did I do that?* I think, *was that me?* I think, *I can do anything.*

I Aitken

Chapter Ten

The violent chemo cocktail of epirubicin and cyclophosphamide was past. I was so overjoyed about having got through this stage, I wanted music playing and balloons released as I left the clinic. Instead, I walked out with no fanfare at all.

I had come through it, though not with my dignity intact. There had been too many rather revolting side effects for me to feel even remotely graceful.

And then I was beset by the menopause.

The. Menopause.

I was 43.

My periods had stopped after the first chemo session; and with their disappearance came the hot flushes and night sweats. My god, the night sweats. Several times a night I would wake in a pool of liquid, drenched through my pyjamas and the sheets. Sleep was broken and unsatisfactory.

During the day, savage hot flushes would engulf me, especially when I came to a halt after having been slightly active; after a walk to the high street, I would enter a shop and pause in front of the shelves. Immediately, flames of heat radiated rapidly up my body and out from my face; trickles of sweat ran down my forehead and settled on my upper lip. This was most disconcerting when someone stopped to speak to me. I could barely focus on what they were saying, I was so painfully aware of my red cheeks and sweaty face.

Dr B had told me, before the worst of it kicked in, "You're still quite young. Menopausal symptoms could disappear at the end of your treatment." And then I would be blessed by the return of my period, before the menopause returned at a more reasonable age. I was slightly relieved and very hopeful, though it did make me understand what it would be like to be full-on climacteric. I would need to carry a fan in my bag at all times, and take ice packs to bed.

One night, while husband hugged me, he jerked away from me as the fieriness bloomed up my body.

"Oh my God," he said. "Are you having a hot flush?"

"Yep," I said proudly.

"That was incredible! I could feel it!"

But it doesn't help that husband's natural resting temperature is akin to that of an oven, and his mere proximity to me can precipitate a hot flush. Hugs in bed are short-lived because of this. "Lie on your side!" I humph in the night, when he has rolled onto my pillow and I am suffused with burning.

If only this energy could be harnessed and used in our central heating.

After seven weeks of the chemotherapy onslaught, I was left unfit and slightly weakened. I was also grumpy, thanks to so much enforced lethargy. Lying around does nothing for one's mental state. But having finished the first course of drugs, I was so relieved, in such good spirits, I was determined to get up and about again, build up my strength, get back to living.

I started on the next course of chemo – 12 weekly shots of Taxol, a drug which husband was very excited about, since it was isolated from the Pacific yew tree. I'm not entirely certain why this is so exciting, but there you go.

Dr B and the chemo nurses assured me that the side effects and impact of Taxol were nothing like those of the first course of drugs, and they would be surprised if I suffered at all.

This was despite them also handing me a leaflet about the side effects, which listed among them nausea and vomiting, loss of appetite, change in taste, thinned or brittle hair, pain in the joints, changes in the colour of the nails, and tingling in the hands or toes.

And that last symptom did appear, the day after my first Taxol session. My fingertips felt like they do after I've chopped chillies – slightly burnt – and doing up buttons was cumbersome and painful. This was apparently due to something called peripheral neuropathy[47], which is basically nerve damage. For the most part, peripheral neuropathy caused by the anticancer drugs disappears at the end of treatment – unless it has got so bad that the nerves cannot mend themselves. The nurses must be told every week how much the neuropathy is affecting you, to allow the oncologist to decide whether to continue with treatment.

But peripheral neuropathy aside… that first day after the new drugs was just amazing. I wasn't stewing in deep sleep. I was awake, and watching Wimbledon on the telly, upright and alert. In the past week, in an attempt to get back into the land of the living, I had gone on a family picnic to the park, to the cinema and to the high street, seven-year-old daughter by my side as an unwitting crutch and emotional support.

With mum visiting to take up her usual chores of laundry and cooking for my family, while I – presumably – would be incapable, we took the children to the Museum of Flight. I hadn't been this active for a couple of months, and it was glorious. I felt alive. I breathed deeply. I took in the colours and the outdoor air.

Of course, I was then floored by exhaustion after so much exertion, which made me feel a bit pathetic. There I was, reading stories about cancer patients running multiple marathons, while I slumped on the sofa in my dressing gown, recovering from a day at the museum.

Pathetic.

The fact that I felt pathetic annoyed me. The fact I was having stories of less pathetic cancer patients thrust in my face also annoyed me. What if all my friends thought I should be able to run marathons too? Would they think I was a cop-out? Weak and spineless? Why couldn't these marathon-running folk keep their fitness prowess to themselves? Such heroic behaviour did nothing for little weaklings like me.

Still, I did manage to take the children to the circus that weekend, and felt only slightly self-conscious as I sat on the ground in the queue to get in, the scarf on my head tied inexpertly and wonkily. Fortunately, I think I looked enough of a state for people to realise I was ill, rather than eccentric.

At the next check-up with Dr B, she asked me, "Do you have any questions about the Taxol?"

"Oh," I said. "Is that why I'm here?" I was so used to having the specialists tell me what was wrong, advise me what to do, inform me what would be happening. I didn't feel the need to ask questions. I couldn't be bothered.

But husband, of course, had several. He scribbled notes as Dr B explained the process from here on.

I shared with Dr B the good news that the Genetic Service had contacted me to say that there were no mutations of my RAD51C and RAD51D genes (which was a pleasant surprise, since I didn't even know, or hadn't remembered, that those were being tested). Such mutations are apparently a predisposition for ovarian cancer, a disease it is believed my grandmother died from. Since there were no mutations in my BRCA1 and BRCA2 genes either, I was now safe in the knowledge that I wasn't a victim of genetically inherited cancer.

"These tests for gene mutations might be negative but there is clearly some other genetic reason for your cancer," said Dr B, rather pissing on my parade. She flicked through my family history, and pointed out that science hadn't necessarily managed to identify all the causes of hereditary cancer, and looking at the abundance of the illness in my family, we were clearly victims of one of the unidentified factors.

So that was nice.

I also mentioned the menopausal symptoms, though. I explained the dire night sweats, the broken sleep patterns. And then Dr B explained that actually, rather than have my periods return after the end of chemo, I would receive treatment to suppress my ovaries and continue the menopause indefinitely.

(Research since that day has made me realise that this was on the assumption my menopause was chemo-related and would disappear at the end of treatment – that my periods would return. Ovarian suppression would block the ovaries from making oestrogen, which, since my breast cancer had been ER+ – in other words, fuelled by oestrogen – was a good idea.)

This news came as something of a surprise, but I seemed to be in no fit intellectual state to process the implications, then and there. That happened two days later, when I suddenly burst into tears.

I was officially an old woman. I didn't want to have any more children, so my infertility now should be meaningless – but it wasn't. To lose my fertility made me redundant, worthless. That's how I felt, anyway. A menopausal woman is one who is in the end stages of her life. She is disrespected by society, laughed at, ignored. She is useless.

I was useless.

My life was being saved but was it even worth it now I was basically old?

The fact that I struggled with this news even more than I had with the cancer itself was slightly odd. Perhaps it was because cancer was an illness that, in my case, had an end in sight. Perhaps it was because cancer had garnered me attention and sympathy. The menopause… well, that was it, wasn't it? No end in sight for that. It *was* the end. And certainly no sympathy, since every bloody woman goes through it, and I've seen how society treats menopausal women.

It seemed so desperately unfair.

This sense of time passing and new episodes in life was reinforced by son finally getting to celebrate his tenth birthday, having had to postpone partying thanks to getting appendicitis five days before he actually turned ten. Husband and I drove six excited boys to the local indoor go-karting track, where they roared round the track, roared through their burger and chips, and roared in the cars coming home again. It was exhausting, for me, if not them, but I watched my boy with such pride. He had successfully navigated his first decade, and was now a funny, thoughtful, caring, sensitive, intelligent, exuberant, enthusiastic young lad.

Still my baby, though.

The Stocking

Though son is my baby, he is of course very much his own person; but there's no mistaking who his dad is. They share the same wide-eyed enthusiasm when talking about their favourite subjects; also vagueness, an inability to just get on with the job in hand, intelligence, sensitivity and kindness. These last virtues son very much inherited from his dad. On one occasion, however, I did come close to hoping son hadn't inherited husband's lack of faithfulness…

Before I was ill, and having made the decision to travel to Asia, a couple of months before, husband went on a fact-finding mission to Japan, combining it with a trip to a conference out there. He was away for a week. When the children had been very small, I found his lengthier work absences hard, as I missed both him and his parental support.

But now the children were older, and were settled into their daily routines. Husband, if truth be told, was hardly missed.

On his return, he (unusually) tipped all the dirty washing from his travel bag into the laundry bin. (Unusual because his habit is to leave the travel bag lying on the bedroom floor for several weeks, allowing everything to fester and rot.)

When it came to laundry day (pah, we don't have a laundry day, don't be ridiculous. The washing gets done when the laundry bin is overflowing and I trip over the clothes to get into bed), I did what is my usual trick of just dragging out the clothes and dividing them into whites, lights and darks. (My mum also does reds, and greens/blues, which I tried for a while, but couldn't be bothered with as it seemed to necessitate even more loads. It's amazing how much of a science laundry is.) I don't check pockets for tissues or pebbles or small pieces of metal, so they invariably go through the wash, too. Why don't I check pockets? I have no idea.

Either I just can't be arsed, or I don't think of it. Husband thinks it is a subconscious obstinacy, since every single wash sees bits of tissue or a sweetie wrapper or some other treasure tumble out the machine.

"Why don't you just check the pockets?" he laughs.

Why don't you do all the f**king laundry, I think.

Anyway, got sidetracked there, sorry. So, I roughly divided the clothing, without any real investigation of the clothing itself. A load of darks was thrust into the machine. A couple of hours later, I unloaded the machine and hung up the laundry.

And it's now that the story becomes interesting (honestly, it does), because among the washing was a black stocking. One. One stocking. A black one.

I haven't worn stockings since before I had children, when I could wear a suspender belt without getting a muffin top.

I hung the stocking on the clothes horse.

I sat down at the kitchen table.

I tried not to vomit.

I wondered how I was going to get through the day until husband came home and I could confront him.

A couple of scenarios ran through my head: 1) He liked to wear women's clothing. Fine, I could deal with that. 2) He had slept with a Japanese prostitute, and accidentally swept her clothing off the floor into his travel bag. It's the sort of thing he would do. Sweep all the clothes off the floor into a bag, I mean, not necessarily sleep with a prostitute. To my knowledge he had not done that so far. But what was to stop him now? So far away from home, alone, (possibly) drunk on Japanese whisky, tired, easily seduced…

I sat at that kitchen table for hours, knowing that I couldn't phone my mum for advice, because it wouldn't be fair to husband not to hear his side of the story first. I considered getting the train into the city and storming his office but, again, I thought it wouldn't be fair to humiliate him in front of his colleagues. My world collapsed in on itself; I was empty, nauseated, and so so alone. I realised I had been taking him for granted; hadn't appreciated how much I loved him.

At last, husband was home. He walked into the kitchen, and I calmly held the stocking aloft.

"I wonder if you could explain who this stocking belongs to and how it came to be in your laundry?" I asked quietly.

Husband stared at the stocking impassively for a couple of seconds, and then burst out laughing.

Well.

A variety of expletives and insults threaded through my mind, but I didn't express them because I was silenced by my bewilderment. How could he laugh at a time like this? I'd caught him out! This was the end of our marriage! And he was laughing?! I shook my head and gawped like a goldfish.

Husband struggled to breathe through his laughter, each of his guffaws stabbing me in the heart.

"That's…" he stammered, "that's… a compression stocking. For long-haul flights."

I Aitken

.

Chapter Eleven

A big part of anyone's survival is the support of friends, family and community.

I was very humbled by my friends' support, because up until my illness I had been feeling increasingly distant from them. I have itchy feet. I get bored quickly, in the same job, in the same house, in the same town. I like to move on.

I had been wanting to move on for a couple of years. I felt myself drifting from the close-knit community around me. I felt as though I had less and less in common with the friends I had made, and as though I was detaching myself from them.

Thank goodness I was unsuccessful.

Their acceptance of spiky little me, and their kind hearts, were evident as soon as I had broken the news of my cancer diagnosis, via a travel blog[48]. Sentiments of sympathy and shock were frequently expressed.

And after the first operation to remove the lump, there were so many bunches of flowers delivered I ran out of vases. That isn't a complaint. I love flowers, and I never get them because husband can't even spell the word romance, let alone indulge in it. He doesn't know the word exists. He doesn't know the concept exists.

I'm not bitter, no.

Anyway, flowers. So many gorgeous spring blooms, scenting the kitchen with their uplifting aromas. And meals! Blimey, the meals. That was such a boon – so many times we would open the front door to find on the doorstep a bag containing boxes of ready cooked meals. On one occasion, mum brought in a bag full of gourmet vegetarian meals, left by a neighbouring friend who knew I had been trying to give up meat. Mum was close to tears at such evidence of thoughtfulness. "This community is incredible," she said.

Since husband didn't really have the time or inclination to cook – and what he did present at mealtimes usually consisted of poached egg and spinach, which didn't do a lot for the constipation – and I didn't have the energy, the donated meals were very gratefully received.

(To this day, I still have two cardboard boxes full of food containers and jars, which have not been returned to their owners.)

Mums offered to take my children to play at their houses after school, and then deliver them home after teatime. My own mum visited frequently, travelling 400 miles each way every time, to wash clothes and dishes, and make sure the children were fed and watered.

I felt nurtured, protected, enclosed in a network of care.

Just ahead of my first operation, my dietician friend asked if she could bake a cake to celebrate getting rid of the cancer. She said I could have whatever sort of cake I liked. I said, any cake? She said yes.

I ordered a boob cake.

It was a commission she fulfilled with aplomb, the cake she brought to my door two days after the operation a scarily accurate replica of a breast, though possibly much pinker. I, on a whim, announced, "Let's have a party!" and so several friends and their children turned up at little notice to witness the cutting of the boob cake.

There was laughter, and gossip, and crudeness, and all-round good humour. It was exhausting but so normal.

And since I was too tired to venture far from the house, friends took it upon themselves to drop by and see if I was up for a chat, sitting with me on deckchairs in the back garden, drinking tea and analysing the world as it turned.

Even better was the Cancer Research UK fundraiser, a cake bake day I hosted, just four days after my second operation. I say I hosted it; literally all I did was give up space in the kitchen for the 20 or 30-odd women (and a couple of men) who came along. The real host was my boob cake pal, who baked a selection of the most gorgeous sponge and fruit concoctions.

The kitchen was heaving with coffee, cake and kind-hearted company. I looked on at the mingling, a post-operation sheen of sweat springing to my face. All I could do was smile and cut cake, failing to engage in any real conversation through sheer lack of energy.

No matter. Thanks to friends' generosity, we raised more than £1300 for Cancer Research UK. My pal and I were astonished.

It made me realise that if there was one thing my particular friends could do, it was donate money to research. It can be hard for friends and family of cancer patients to know what to do. They feel helpless and powerless, but desperately want to do something. Anything. Hence the bunches of flowers and ready cooked meals. These were practical, functional offerings that they knew might make a difference.

With the opportunity to eat cake and raise money to fight cancer at the same time, boob cake pal and I had given them another means to support me and other cancer patients – another sense of helping, of having some control over the shitness.

After those first seven or eight weeks of toxic chemo, though, and once I was on the less brutal Taxol, my energy began to return. The cooked meals thinned out, though they didn't disappear entirely. Husband began to cook, using the ingredients and recipes provided by a subscription food delivery service.

I began to venture further and further from home, desperate to enter real life again. So I was still a bit tired. So I was beset by hot flushes. (In fact, I was besieged by a long list of irritating but just-about-bearable side effects: hair loss, nose bleeds, change in taste, mouth ulcers, peripheral neuropathy, sore nails, exhaustion, breathlessness, dry skin, oedema[49]...). But that didn't stop me from planning all sorts of outings and entertainment.

First up was the annual week-long music & arts festival in my home town. Every year for the previous nine years of its existence I had gone along to enjoy musicians and comedians I would otherwise not see. Every year the festival was bigger and better. This year was no different, and I saw it as a celebration of my return to the land of the living.

Blazing through the tiredness, I summoned the will and the energy to meander down to the spiegeltents at the harbour to watch a variety of entertainment: rocking KT Tunstall, scathing Zoe Lyons, unorthodox Richard Herring, and the brilliant Aly Bain & Phil Cunningham; a fondly comical skit about the Famous Five by a local theatre group; fabulous Scottish/Indian dance group Dance Ihayami; and "acoustic mash-up" band Banjo Lounge 4, who rather wonderfully provided versions of hip hop, electronica and rock songs on banjo, guitar and double bass. Imagine Underworld's Born Slippy in three-part harmony.

By the end of the week I was exhausted and so very happy.

Dad popped up to visit us for a few days; actually, visiting us was incidental to the reason he usually pops up to Scotland, which is to visit his siblings or play golf. Sometimes both. We provide the free accommodation, so he has to put up with us, too.

When he arrived, I was in bed; he stuck his head round the bedroom door to say hi and, to be fair to him, reacted pretty well to my baldness, though he did giggle.

"It's like looking in a mirror, isn't it?" I said, one eyebrow raised*.

And the entertainment didn't stop there, oh no. Since moving to Scotland, I have also been a regular attendee at the Edinburgh Book Festival, and I was damned if I would miss it this year.

Books are my oxygen. The Edinburgh Book Festival is my... oxygen tank. I revel in the civilised atmosphere of learning; but I'm an embarrassing fan girl when it comes to meeting my literary heroes. I could not give a toss about the royal family or reality TV stars; but present me with an author and my eyes shine and I start giggling.

My first event was with Scottish makar** Jackie Kay[50]. The previous year I had seen Jackie in conversation with First Minister Nicola Sturgeon[51], and that had been possibly the best and happiest hour of my life: two incredibly intelligent and amusing women, sharing their love of literature in front of an intrigued audience.

This year Jackie was alone, talking about the centenary of World War One poets Wilfred Owen and Siegfried Sassoon having met in Edinburgh's Craiglockhart Hospital. She mentioned her grandfather, who had also fought in the War, and who had sustained such injuries that he ended up carrying a large piece of shrapnel in his arm for years afterwards. This eventually worked its own way out, his body finally ejecting the metal.

"I like to think of that piece of shrapnel as a story held by his body," said Jackie, a whimsical view that immediately resonated with me. That's what my cancer is, I thought. A story, author unknown, germinating and

* I didn't – I can't raise one eyebrow.
** The Scottish poet laureate

growing in my body.

Or, rather, just one chapter, with any luck, in the story of my life.

Next at the festival were Peter Høeg and Michelle Paver in conversation. I had been a die-hard fan of Peter's since I read *Miss Smilla's Feeling For Snow* at university, the book's enigmatic female hero an inspiration. I didn't know Michelle – and that's what I love about the Book Festival. When I go to see an author I know and admire in conversation, I am invariably introduced to another author whose work I then buy and enjoy. I was entranced by Peter, his existence almost legendary for me.

"My translator needs to be arrogant," he said. "He has to read my book and then write the English version as if there never was an original and it is his." And that analogy of my cancer being a story chapter returned to me; now I compared Peter's translator with my consultant and oncologist, who needed a certain arrogance to take my body and rewrite the cancer chapter into something more legible, more acceptable.

I thought about all those other cancer patients I encountered in clinic, and the stories they told the chemo nurses. One old gent would weekly inform the nurse that he was incapable of keeping food down, no matter how much they jiggled the anti-sickness drugs. His oedema was also unbearable, and he needed regular massages to relieve the swelling round his ankles.

A woman patient was proud to say that she had been able to do some gardening the previous week – imagine feeling relieved that you have the energy to do a bit of weeding. (Not that gardening is easy, of course. I still get knackered pulling up dandelions.)

Curtains were pulled round the treatment chair when a patient could no longer hold in the tears. They would sob out their frustration and fears; of course we could hear this, and sympathise, but there's something about weakness that needs dignity and privacy. Weakness! As if struggling with sodding cancer is weak.

But all these stories – of symptoms, side effects and suffering – could anyone have foreseen them? The patients certainly wouldn't have added this chapter to the tale of their lives. Who took over authorship? To have control of your story taken away is breathtakingly bewildering. And then you hand over the rewriting and editing to the medical experts, hoping that they pay attention to house style and stick to the script you were creating before cancer barged in.

The last Book Festival event I made it to was with comedian Sara Pascoe. She was there to promote (of course!) her book, *Animal: The Autobiography Of A Female Body*. I sat on the end of the row, scarf on my head to cover my self-conscious baldness, bottle of water in one hand and fan in the other. A young woman sat beside me and asked, "Do you have cancer?" I said yes, but before I could marvel at her observation or her bluntness, she explained that her mum also had cancer, so she recognised all the accoutrements.

Sara was very funny. *Animal* is a catalogue of the female body, biology and experiences, in all their seriousness, sensitivity and comedy. It is both memoir and evolutionary history, detailing what it is to be a sexual female. She related her own horrible experiences to a hushed audience; and also drew laughter with her self-effacement.

After the talk, I lined up to have my book signed and my photo taken with Sara. She, unlike all other authors, came out from behind her desk to stand by me with her arm around my shoulder. I was so self-conscious about my sweatiness, my red cheeks and wonky head scarf, I felt I had to justify it all by suggesting she write her next book on the menopause. I guess I'll have to wait 20 years before she actually goes through it.

Talking of being self-conscious…

Losing one's hair, so suddenly and so completely, is akin to losing one's identity. Eyebrows and eye lashes all but disappear – one is almost featureless. The Look Good Feel Better volunteers at Edinburgh's Maggie's Centre knew this, and were generous with their time and make-up expertise, showing us how to draw on eyebrows and effectively moisturise drying skin, among other cosmetic tips.

I decided to take what I had learned from them and do a YouTube makeover[52], *à la* Zoella[53] and Sprinkle of Glitter[54] – except mine ended up not being quite as sincere as theirs.

The motive for making this video was complex: just as one is not in control of the cancer that takes over one's life, so one is no longer in control of one's image. Is it only women who would feel like this? I don't think so. I think men are just as concerned when they start losing hair. Although, maybe because that's a sign of their mortality, rather than a fear of the way they look? Perhaps that's a discussion for another, more academic book. Personally, as someone who had often used my hairstyle and colour to express an image, a character, having none at all was somewhat disheartening. I handled it better than I could have done, after the initial shock of clumps of hair coming away in my hands; in fact, it's only now, when I look back at the video, that I realise just how odd I looked, with a shiny billiard ball head and the portacath sticking out from above my chest. When it's actually happening to you, at the time, you are shocked by it but you're still you, inside. At first glance, I think other people don't realise that. So, I understood the need for cancer patients to get back to some physical semblance of the "real them", and take back control of their image.

The other reason for doing this makeover video was because there is a propensity for such things, and often what they achieve is to make some women feel worse about themselves. What's wrong with wearing no make-up on the school run? What's the matter with looking a bit tired when you are a bit tired? Of course, I'm as much a victim of this vanity as anyone. Like many women, I see wearing make-up as a mask, a costume for a character who can take on the world and win. Though I do go make-up free much more often these days, it does leave me feeling vulnerable and unattractive. Which is not the fault of YouTube makeover videos, but still. I wanted to satirise the desperate need to conform to beauty – especially when one is being treated for cancer. Really, one has more important things to think about than contouring.

Book Festival jollity over, an old schoolfriend travelled up to stay for a few nights, both to visit me and to take a breather from her own relentless routine. We sat in the sun on deckchairs, drinking tea and gossiping. I worried she'd be bored, so suggested we go for a walk down to the sea and along the beach for a bit.

"Are you sure you've got the energy?" asked schoolfriend. I assured her that we wouldn't be going far, and I was absolutely fine to walk these days.

Well, obviously I overestimated how fit I was, and underestimated just how tired my body was.

It was a hot day. The air was all sunlight and holiday atmosphere. Only 10 minutes into the walk along the beach, I could feel my legs officially resigning. This kind of physical exhaustion is quite vexing – it's not just a simple case of feeling tired, of having aching muscles. It's the unnerving sensation of having no energy at all in one's legs; of the brain's command to move just not making it down the nervous system. Or, if the message is getting there, the legs ignoring it. Or being unable to obey it. Or something. Anyway, frightened I would simply drop to the ground, I struggled to find a bench and sit down, while schoolfriend ran off to the putting green hut to see if the greenkeeper had some water. I was so uncomfortably hot by this stage, I slid my wig off, and sat embarrassed but defiant in all my bald glory. Several other walkers and golfers wandered by and all of them ignored me. Not a batted eyelid in sight.

Schoolfriend ran back with some water and I gratefully knocked it back. One woman did stop to ask if I was okay, explaining that she was a retired nurse, and if I needed anything she lived nearby.

Another plunge forwards took schoolfriend and I into a nearby hotel, where I sat in the mercifully cool air-conditioned lobby while she ran home to fetch her car and return to pick me up.

The tiredness was frustrating, and did nothing for my increasingly unstable emotions. Feeling unattractive is immensely demoralising and undermining. One feels diminished. Especially when one flirts, as usual, then sees the expression on, for example, a young waiter's face and sees oneself through his eyes… A sweaty, bald, middle-aged woman, fluttering her lash-free eyelids. And with the intensifying fatigue, I felt more and more powerless. Crying at nothing became common; I didn't really understand the comments from friends, who called me inspirational and brave. I didn't feel at all inspirational or brave. I felt ugly and old.

The Naïvety

I was late to sex. Or sex was late to me. I suffered the most incapacitating self-consciousness into my early 20s, was embarrassed by my flat chest and unfeminine, curveless shape. When I was 13, at a youth club one Saturday morning, some sort of game of chase in a darkened room led to a lad in the year above me at school thrusting his hands up my top and grasping at my chest (that wasn't the aim of the game at all). "There's nothing there!" he expostulated, the disdain in his voice so acute it cut through my childhood innocence and made me suddenly, painfully, chokingly aware of what I should be, what I should look like, what was expected of me.

Throughout my teens and into university I hid my torso in baggy men's shirts. Hid my face behind a thick curtain of hair. Hid my lack of self-confidence with a sharp tongue and a well-aimed kick at the balls of any lad foolish enough to tease me.

Plenty of snogging throughout university led no further. As time went on but my relationship skills didn't, I became even more self-conscious, concerned that my lack of experience would humiliate me if and when the opportunity to bump and grind arose.

And then something odd happened. I became attractive. I have no idea how or why. I didn't change, I didn't make an overt decision to tone down my aggression. But I hit 23 years old and was suddenly batting men off like swatting mosquitoes.

Of course I wasn't. I was so unused to having male attention, so accustomed to being thought of as an unfeminine freak ("Oh, I thought you were going to be pretty," a man once said as he overtook me and peered at my face), that I thought this positive male gaze was flattering. I'm ashamed to say I giggled when the man at the train station told me I was attractive. I felt powerful and intoxicated with a previously unknown allure when the man in the nightclub grabbed me, kissed me and told me I was beautiful.

Jesus.

I can't imagine, now, thinking that those men's behaviour was okay. I wasn't self-confident or sure enough of myself to understand that though their enormous sense of proprietorship was essentially benign in those cases, it was still unnecessary, irrelevant. Why did I give a shit how attractive they thought I was? I didn't know any of them. Their opinion of me should not have had any import, should have had no impact on my mood or self-esteem.

Look, it is one thing to appreciate beauty. It is quite another for a man with a clearly sexual agenda to tell a woman they do not know, whom they have never seen before, that she is beautiful. Touching her with familiarity, no matter how gently or blamelessly, is not flattery. It is not harmless. It is unremittingly inapposite. Men's general opinion of a woman's aesthetics means nothing. It will not make her more important a person or more successful; it does not validate her existence. Unfortunately, when you're young and self-conscious and somewhat lacking in self-esteem, you don't realise this.

Anyway, my own giggling naivety kind of got me into a position I came to regret but which fortunately did not end up as horrific as it could have been.

Remember that journalism NVQ? The one based in lively metropolis, Mitcham? The course involved three separate weeks of work experience. I did a week at the *West Sussex County Times*, a week on *Financial Times How To Spend It* magazine and a week at a title that shall remain nameless, since it's where the production editor took a shine to little old me, and grasped the opportunity to take me down to the basement "to do some photocopying" and then snog me.

I was hugely flattered. He was 10 years my senior, with long, lustrous, dark brown hair and Latin good looks. I had never been swept off my feet in this way, certainly not by anyone sober.

He suggested I head over to his flat in south London the Sunday evening at the end of my work experience week, for a drink and a chat, go out to a bar… I genuinely thought that's all he would expect. I felt sophisticated and slightly conceited.

But we didn't go out. He suggested we stay in and watch a film. He also suggested I stay the night but I didn't want to, since the next day I was to start my week at the *Financial Times*. I wanted to get back to my mate's house, where I was staying, to have a good night's sleep, to prepare myself for my week at one of the world's best newspapers.

But it got later and later, and somehow I didn't fancy the idea of travelling back across London on public transport. Eventually I conceded that staying the night might be an idea, as long as he could drive me back to my mate's in the morning, on his way to work. "I'll sleep on the sofa," I said, an uneasiness about my lack of experience kicking in. I fancied him, a bit, but I knew he wasn't the one to pop my cherry. The vampish, devil-may-care behaviour I had exhibited in the office was rapidly ebbing away, overtaken by the realisation that that just wasn't me, I wasn't a flirt, I didn't know what to do next, I didn't want to…

"No," he said. "I'll sleep on the sofa, and you can take the bed." I almost threw up with relief.

But when I exited the bathroom a little later, and made my way to his bedroom, there he was, apparently naked in his bed.

"Oh," I stopped and turned. I knew then that I had been tricked. I knew then that I was in a situation I desperately wanted to escape. So why didn't I just leave?

I have absolutely no idea.

"Come on," he said, "it's fine, don't be daft. I won't do anything."

Oh my god, I felt such a fool. A fool to have got myself into this position, and an even bigger fool for not knowing how to get out of it. I didn't want him to think I was inexperienced, I didn't want him to think I didn't know what I was doing… I didn't want to seem young, innocent and ignorant.

I climbed into the bed.

This is harder to write than I thought it would be.

I don't want to paint this man as some sort of villain. He was a sleazebag, yes, but ultimately he had a powerful sense of what was right and wrong, because though his promise not to "do anything" wasn't strictly true, at the point where he was lying above me, over me, his naked body the clearest sign yet of where he wanted this to go, his gentle swaying and what he thought was a teasing smile – "oo, look at this…" – an assumption that I wanted to go there too… though he went as far as he could… he got the message. I was frozen. I lay still, my limbs rigid. I stared up into his face, and he must have seen the terror, the weakness, because he stopped. He lay down and went to sleep.

I was locked into an almost foetal position all night and didn't close my eyes once.

The next morning he drove me back to my friend's house, and I washed, dressed and got the train back to Southwark, my exhaustion, humiliation and shame suppressed by a suit and professional smile.

Chapter Twelve

I continued to fight the weariness and impotence, and suggested a visit to Bangour Village Hospital[55]. Ought to explain this one – I've been writing a novel for years now, constantly editing, unpicking and rewriting. Part of it is set in World War Two, and part of the World War Two bit is set in Bangour Village Hospital.

Between the two World Wars it was a psychiatric hospital, comprising villas, its own railway connection, a farm, bakery, workshops, recreation hall, school, shop, library and church – a village – but during both Wars it was requisitioned and became a military hospital; specialising in burns and plastic surgery from 1940.

I had learned about it as part of my book research, and written about it from my imagination. Now I learned that the hospital grounds, closed since 2004, were up for sale, and due to be redeveloped for residential use. I was desperate to see the remains of the hospital before they disappeared.

Accordingly, we packed the children into the car and set off, promising them an adventure. And it really was, though perhaps not one they had envisioned. The site of the hospital sprawls over 960 acres, a collection of villas and buildings widely spaced apart. They are falling into wrack and ruin now, but peeking through smashed windows one sees the peeling paint and fallen chairs of an abandoned hospital.

On its hilly position, looking down over vast grassy fields and across to the trees that hide the M8, and on a grey cloudy day, as it was when we visited, I swear one can feel the energy of the patients who have stayed there, aided by the fact that evidence of their existence, such as a bus stop and paperwork strewn on the hospital floors, still exist.

We trekked around the four miles of roadways through the grounds, peering through windows, occasionally passing dog walkers and being regularly passed by the patrolling security guards. There was something almost Wuthering Heights about the place – windswept and wildly emotive.

The children dashed on their scooters along the roads, exploring pathways and scaring themselves with talk of ghosts. The crumbling buildings were a sorry sight; such magnificent edifices that had served for so long, abandoned and uncared for, an eerie "knock knock" graffitied on one patched up wooden door reinforcing the sense of neglect.

After a couple of hours investigating the hospital, I had had enough of being active. I stumbled back to the car, tired but touched by the thought of those who had lived and worked here.

A couple of weeks later, yet another chemo side-effect showed up, when my face suddenly went red, hot and blotchy. I called the chemo clinic.

"I've got a rash on my face," I told GH. "I look like a pizza."

"Okay. Do you have a temperature?"

"No."

"What is your temperature?"

"I don't know but it was fine the last time I took it."

"When did you take it?"

"Three weeks ago."

Of course, this prompted a telling-off, since I was supposed to be checking my temperature a lot more regularly. Any deviance could signal illness or infection and would need to be reported immediately. GH made me take my temperature while she waited on the phone.

It was absolutely normal, but she told me to see my GP that day, which is a surprisingly easy thing to do when you're having chemo. So many complaints these days by people saying they can never get a doctor's appointment – actually, if you're ill and vulnerable, the NHS will prioritise you.

The GP, when I saw him that afternoon, barely gave me a glance before diagnosing rosacea. Rosacea! That was one affliction I hadn't been expecting. The antibiotic gel I was prescribed cooled down and soothed the burning sensation, though once it had dried it peeled off my face, which looked as though I had some form of leprosy. Incredibly, none of the friends I saw before I realised my face was peeling off said anything, showing that, when it came to cancer, they would accept every way in which I was affected without question.

On top of the rosacea came the announcement by daughter one day that she had a sore toe. We took a look, and concluded from its redness that it was probably infected. She would need to go to the doctor the next day. That evening, she threw up; husband and I panicked that she had sepsis. On top of the panic came the muted but very real sense that I had had enough of this sort of shit. I mean, children invariably come down with illnesses and are inflicted by injuries, but really? Could it not have been put on hold until I was cured of cancer?

Several calls to NHS24 reduced the panic to a mere simmer, and daughter slept with me that night, her every sudden movement (and boy, does she move suddenly when she's asleep – she punched me in the face at one point) hauling me from a light sleep to check she was okay.

The next day was chemo day – I explained to DE that the reason I was so exhausted was because my sick child had kept me awake all night.

"Wait," she said, "the sick child slept with the chemo patient?" and she looked pointedly at husband. He slept with daughter that night; and it turned out that she had both a toe infection and a tummy bug, independent of each other but coincidentally at the same time.

By now the end of chemo was in sight. Just two more sessions to go, and I would be welcoming back my hair and saying goodbye to all the side effects. I'd be cured, too, of course. It was easy to forget the cancer because that had never given me any problems – it was the treatment that was such hard work and so invasive. The tunnel I had travelled down had been long and seemingly continuous, but now I could see the light at the end of it, dim and distant but definitely there.

At my penultimate chemo session, the nurses, as usual, asked after my peripheral neuropathy. The extent of the numbness in my fingers would have an impact on whether my treatment would be interrupted or continued. I explained that it had reached further than ever, nearly halfway down my fingers, a strange tingling numbness that made doing up laces and buttons nigh on impossible. It also made cooking even more hazardous, since I couldn't feel heat or cold, and was at risk of burning my fingers without noticing.

"Hmm," said the nurse. "We'll mention it to Dr B, and she'll decide whether to reduce the chemo dosage or delay the final session."

"Delay the final session?" I asked, feeling mutinous. Suddenly that tunnel seemed to have stretched again, the light at the end of it grown even more dim. When you are submitting yourself to such an endurance, when you are willing yourself to cope until a fixed date, to have that date extended whips away the tentative courage and resignation that underpins your existence.

"Well, if the last session is delayed, I won't turn up for it at all," I said petulantly. The nurse said nothing.

Five days later, just two days before I was due in for my now unconfirmed last chemo session, I received a call from nurse IJ. "You know when you were last in," he said, "and your peripheral neuropathy had progressed? And we said that Dr B would make the decision as to whether to delay the final session, or reduce the dosage?"

I held my breath.

"Well," continued IJ, "Dr B has said to miss the final session entirely. But we still want you to come in on Thursday! We need to take bloods and things."

Wait, what? Yes, yes, bloods, of course. But…

"I won't have this session at all?" I said quickly, breathlessly. "It won't be delayed? Last Thursday was my last session and I don't have to have any more chemo?"

"That's right," said IJ. Relief thundered through my soul like a tidal wave of emotion. I was released from a sort of torture. I felt suddenly light.

But, of course, what goes up must come down (unless it's a satellite or space junk, as son has pointed out). That final Thursday I returned to the clinic, but this time just to have my bloods taken, and to hand out party bags to the nurses and staff. I felt in a celebratory mood, but there were other patients just starting and still enduring their treatment, so the atmosphere was muted.

As the days went on, I couldn't understand why I wasn't feeling so much better already. With the end of chemo should come the immediate end of all the side effects, surely? Of course not, that's not how it works. But it's very hard to endure the signs and symptoms of chemo once it's over, it's behind you, you want to forget about it.

It didn't help that I was also becoming more and more emotional, a state I was blaming on the fact I had stopped taking fluoxetine, an anti-depressant, at the beginning of the summer, since Dr B had said it would clash with the tamoxifen I would soon be taking. It's one thing to come off anti-depressants – it's quite another to do so just before plunging into the (chemo-induced) menopause, with all the mentally challenging aspects that that entails.

I would burst into tears at the drop of a hat, over nothing. Music, which has always affected me, would fell me. Adverts for charities left me bereft. *Comedies* left me emotionally unstable. It was so tiring.

But, even so, I was determined to claw back some semblance of normal life. I began walking daughter to school again, panting with pain and pride at the top of the hill, engaging in all the wonderfully banal conversations with other mums (I had so missed those); husband and I went to a dinner-and-dance fundraiser for the school, though I only managed to eat and chat my way through the three-course meal before I had to bail out just as the dancing started, and stumble home.

Such small yet challenging steps. But that was the first, hardest part over. Now I was alert, aware, of my immediate surroundings, the children's moods and needs and, more interestingly, the events of the wider world…

I Aitken

The Anger

My life until now had been fuelled by passion, and often anger. I have an overdeveloped sense of injustice. I had revelled in being first a pain in the arse about this at school and then, with the invention of the interweb and social media, a prolific keyboard warrior. Just in case no-one noticed the inequities in life, I was there to point them out. (As if anyone was listening to little old me.) And 2017 was quite the year for injustice – but, unfortunately for me and my sense of unfairness, I was only semi-conscious throughout.

Look, the coming paragraphs are going to sound very self-centred. If you don't hate me already, you will.

Wallowing down there in the post-chemo murk, I was selfish and thoughtless. Actually, to be selfish would be to assume some sort of conscious thought. And I wasn't consciously thinking. I was asleep, even when I was awake. I was absent, apathetic. My brain didn't have the time or energy for empathy and certainly not critical thinking. It was too busy trying to deal with the shock of poison coursing through my body, and working hard to eradicate it.

The first of the overwhelmingly awful events of 2017 was the Westminster attack[56] on 22nd March; Khalid Masood drove a car into pedestrians and then stabbed an unarmed police officer. Described by police as Islamist-related terrorism, there was nevertheless a disconnect between the event and the way I felt about it, due not only to its geographical distance from me but also to the fact that I had only just returned from Tokyo with my breast cancer diagnosis. My head was a whirlwind of emotions, and I had precious few spare for this horrible attack.

When the Manchester Arena bombing[57] occurred on 22nd May,

however, I was almost fully surfaced from my first chemo session. I was able to experience shock and sympathy. I cried heartbroken tears for the victims, so many so young. I even had enough energy to be outraged by media overreactions, by US security leaks, by the immediate assumptions of terrorism and ensuing Islamophobic attacks. I was briefly aroused from all thoughts of cancer by the semantics of terrorism, my anger at the British Government's response. I was capable – and, perversely, glad – of grief.

But when the London Bridge attack[58] came, on 3rd June, I was barely aware of it. Someone might have mentioned it – I certainly wasn't watching the news. I was in bed, or sleeping on the sofa downstairs. Drifting up a couple of days later I became more conscious of the event, and felt as though I had missed out on all the crucial data and debate. I resented being out-of-date and behind. I despaired at having to formulate my opinions so long after the event; long enough that they were no longer relevant and not worth sharing on social media.

Such resentment was entirely inappropriate, of course. What I thought of these tragedies, their impact on me, was entirely immaterial. To have such self-pity in these moments was selfish and self-obsessed. Oh, but I was so enraged by my impotence! I couldn't believe the world was still turning without me, such atrocities were occurring without me being able to condemn them! Without me even being aware of them!

And then, on 14th June, on the day of my last noxious, brutal epirubicin/cyclophosphamide session, Grenfell Tower[59] burned down. Though the official number of deaths stands at 72, there must be many more unaccounted for. The fire raged while I was unconscious, sleeping off the toxins. But the tragedy burned on throughout the summer, pulling me out of my own self-pity, redirecting my sympathy towards the victims, my ire at the authorities.

I'm not glad of this, of course I'm not. I wasn't relieved that these disasters gave me something else to think about. If that's the impression I give, that's my fault for expressing myself so unclearly. It's hard to explain how one feels when one is weak, ill, tired and powerless, but confronted by circumstances which would normally merit a fervent desire for activism and change.

I was so aggrieved, but could barely even cry; I couldn't even summon the energy to expel teardrops from my tired eyes.

I was frustrated. Frustrated by the tragedies. Frustrated by what caused them. Frustrated by their consequences. And angry that there was nothing I could do with this frustration.

I Aitken

Chapter Thirteen

A n end-of-chemo appointment with Dr B had her outlining my prognosis and explaining what treatment would be yet to come. I would take tamoxifen to block oestrogen and prevent the cancer returning. (Basically, my cancer cells required oestrogen to grow and reproduce. Tamoxifen[60] mimics oestrogen and binds with the oestrogen receptors in the breast cancer cells – deceiving them. By blocking the binding of oestrogen with the cancer cells, tamoxifen can halt the cancer's growth. Terribly clever stuff. Reassuringly, this meant I wouldn't turn into a man after all.) If my periods returned, I would be given Zoladex[61], an ovary-suppressant. This would then necessitate Zometa, a drug to strengthen the bones and prevent bone cancer. It was a list of procedures and ongoing treatment. For a cancer patient, the journey can continue, long after the cancer is gone.

"The chemo drugs have left your body three weeks after treatment," drawled Dr B, which gave me the instant and possibly unrealistic hope that on precisely the 21st day after my last chemo session, my hair would grow back and I would feel great.

Broaching the subject of the night sweats that woke me several times nightly, Dr B said she would prescribe me citalopram, an anti-anxiety drug which has the unlicensed but rather wonderful side effect of reducing the impact and severity of hot flushes[62].

Husband and I left Dr B's office, returned to the waiting room, and were soon called into Mr A's room, where he went over the details of the third and final operation I would be having – a lymphectomy. This would entail a full axilla clearance (all the lymph nodes in my right armpit removed), the chemo portacath removed from under my skin, and liposuction to remove fat from my belly and insert it into my breast, in an attempt to plump it up a bit.

Looking back now, that's quite a procedure. At the time I was completely unfazed. More than anything, I wanted that damn port out of my body.

Dr B's assertion that chemo leaves the body after three weeks, and my optimism that the side effects would disappear, were upheld by my tastebuds returning a month after the end of chemo. They were mending themselves and restoring my ability to actually savour food; to taste the differences, to salivate over sweetness, pucker up with sour, relish salt.

I would walk down to the high street and raid the deli for pots of tomato & feta salad, the tomato tang and feta pungency rolling around my mouth, an ecstasy of sensation.

No longer was eating just a necessity, a fuel, a chore that had to be done. The metallic essence of off-yogurt drifted away, leaving all the true piquancy of food. And this ecstasy of flavour returned in the autumn, just at that season when my body craves stodge, wanting to fatten up for the winter months. (That is totally a thing.)

This revelation and return to the norm was delightful; a sign of positive things to come...

The week before the op I arrived at hospital for a health assessment, and was greeted in the waiting room by chemo nurse MO. "We miss you!" she said. "We almost called you on Thursday morning to say hello." If they had called me, I would have immediately panicked, assuming I had missed an appointment. Chemo clinic had been such a part of my routine for nearly five months, it was proving strangely difficult getting used to not going.

"You made it look so easy!" continued MO, and this odd comment lit up like a neon sign at the front of my cerebral cortex. Easy. I had made it look easy. Our light-hearted conversation about the weather and my treatment and her career progression continued while I silently unpicked her statement.

It had been easy – hadn't it? The impact of chemo is pretty dire, but the process itself isn't so bad, not really. You literally turn up, sit in a chair and let the nurses take over. You itemise your niggles and frustrations and have the nurses nod in passive sympathy or bestow experienced advice. Simple. And that weekly trip into clinic for the Taxol had been a welcome break from boring routine at home, an escape from the confines of walls I could see with my eyes closed. Bed was boring. Home was humdrum. A jaunt into town to see different faces and hear new conversations was positively uplifting.

And then I thought, maybe it was easy for me because I wasn't suffering as much as so many other people. I remembered the old man who couldn't keep food down, and the woman crying behind closed curtains, worn down with weakness. When push came to shove, my life was going through a difficult phase but I knew it would come to a conclusion. The light at the end of that ominously dark tunnel was faint but definitely there. The side effects of chemo, for me, had been largely irritating; it was very much worse for some other people. Unbearable, in fact.

Two nurses conducted the pre-op assessment in a tiny room tucked away in a corner of the hospital. Over the course of an hour, one bombarded me with rapid-fire questions as to my health and wellbeing, while the other took blood, an ECG, and a vial of urine (well, I mean, I filled a vial with urine and she took that off me. Not that she took the urine from me like she did the blood. Never mind, carry on). It was remarkably intense, and focusing on both of them at the same time was impossible – I took to alternating my attention between the two, and then failing to respond promptly or correctly.

And then one of them made me laugh and I farted. I said excuse me and was momentarily embarrassed before assuring myself that these were nurses – they would have encountered far worse than an innocent little pump. They said nothing and my embarrassment drifted away with the gas.

But the following week was not devoid of negative emotions. Regardless of the fact I had been through this process of being operated on twice previously, and despite the fact the procedure had always gone well, I became anxious about this third and final operation.

I didn't think anything would go wrong; but I frequently had flashbacks of waking up on the recovery ward, oxygen mask over my face; or being alone in my room, waiting for a nurse to come and help me to the toilet. Even though I had not suffered or been afraid during those actual moments, it was the mere memory that made my stomach churn now; the sudden and vividly coloured recollections.

This was pretty infuriating. I've done this before, I thought. It's a piece of cake! But it seems that I am less scared of the unknown – once I know what's going on, my anxiety runs away with my imagination and concocts a scenario of fear.

Still, my post-chemo energy was returning, thankfully, so I was able to distract myself by taking mum and the children out to local museums, and, most excitingly, to Alnwick Castle[63], seeking dragons and slaying enemy knights.

(Talking of slaying the enemy – I'd just like to repeat my intense antipathy to the expression "battling cancer". It peed me off right from the start of my own illness; it hadn't been a saying I thought much about when I'd seen it (over)used in the media – *such-and-such a celebrity has lost their battle with cancer* – except that I do remember thinking it was a bit unfair to imply that, by dying, the patient was a loser. The problem with the "battling" metaphor is that patients really don't. Battle, that is. One's body allows a mutation to seed itself, to spread and destroy one's healthy cells. There is no battle. My own breast was blissfully unaware of the cancerous intruder invading and making itself at home. It's the surgeons who engage in war, and one's body becomes merely a battle ground. It's a surprisingly passive process on the patient's part. I would say a cancer patient lives with the disease. Lives with not only the disease but all the treatments and the side effects that come with those treatments, and the battle that the scientists and doctors are engaging in.

Rather than losing their battle with cancer, patients merely die from the disease. Stop implying weakness, lack of courage, and failure on their part.)

Anyway. As I made my way through the hospital to my room for the third and final op, it was indeed a familiar process that didn't at all merit being anxious. I almost sighed with ennui as I sat down on the bed, and threw my bag onto the chair in the corner. The nurse came in to go over the procedure, followed by a reassuringly suave anaesthetist.

I asked the anaesthetist if it would be possible for him to put the cannula in my arm, as had been done in my first operation, rather than in my hand, as in the second, as the hand had hurt more. He said he would do what he could.

Then Mr A joined me to reiterate the procedure, and I signed the usual papers and nodded in weary understanding.

My anxiety, however, did rear its head a little when the nurse who came to take me to theatre insisted I wear a dressing gown and slippers. I didn't see why I should, and hadn't brought any slippers with me. I was unnecessarily snippy, but quietened down when the nurse presented me with a hospital gown and slippers. I followed her meekly to the anaesthetist's room.

The suave anaesthetist told me to clench and unclench my dehydrated hand, as he sought a buried vein. The assistant gently removed my right arm from the gown, which ceased the clenching in my left fist.

"Keep clenching, don't stop!" said the anaesthetist, urgently.

"Sorry," I replied, "I was just listening to your assistant."

"You should be able to do two things at once!" said the anaesthetist. "Women can do that."

"Multi-tasking is a fallacy," I said, righteously, "And some men struggle to do *one* thing at a time."

(Quick pause – multi-tasking is a fallacy, you know, and the ability to do so is beyond most men and women. We might be required to juggle many things but there are only as many balls in your hands as you have hands… wait, I'm just going to abandon that analogy, it's confusing me. What I mean is, you can only concentrate on one thing at a time. You think you're doing many things simultaneously, but actually what you're doing is focusing on one thing after another in quick succession. What about a Red Arrows pilot, you ask, they have to concentrate on loads of things at once, don't they? Not really – they learn to perform a sequence of movements or skills extremely quickly, which become one pattern. This is why it's illegal to use a mobile phone while driving, even for Red Arrow pilots – it is impossible to do so safely. (I just made all that up. I'm going to check… Gah. Apparently there is such a thing as a supertasker[64], someone whose brain functions more efficiently than most, who can be found in jobs such as chef, racing driver and… fighter pilot. But they account for only 2.5% of the population so I stand by my homebaked theory.) (Also, yes, I was joking about men being rubbish at multitasking, some women struggle to do one thing at a time, too, get over it.))

"Well, I am trying to find a vein in your arm, rather than one in your hand, which is what you wanted," replied the anaesthetist. (Yes, we're back there again. Keep up.)

"He's doing as he's asked!" said the (female) assistant. "That makes a change."

"Men always get the last word," said the anaesthetist.

"No they don't," said his assistant.

"They do."

"They don't."

"Yes, darling."

We all laughed. Then everything went black.

I woke in the recovery ward, this time with no oxygen mask shrouding my face. A nurse asked if I wanted my glasses on and I merely grunted in reply – my eyes were open but I was as yet too dazed to focus or think coherently.

I don't remember being wheeled back to my room, or husband rejoining me there from the little sitting room where he sat to work or watch television while I was operated on.

I quickly recovered alertness, though, and chatted quietly with husband, eventually persuading him to go home so he could put the children to bed. Once he was gone, I snoozed as I floated on the raft of drugs in my system.

A few hours later my stomach was grumbly enough to warrant food, so the egg sandwich I had pre-ordered was fetched and I gobbled it down. Big mistake. That egg sandwich sat heavy in my stomach, a ball of stodge that goaded me. I grew hotter and hotter in the tiny room, under smothering blankets and the IPC device which trapped me in the bed. I sipped frequently from the glass of water at my bedside – also a mistake, since the egg sandwich stodge ball was now a bulky, floating mass, expanding in my uncomfortable body.

I rang for the nurse. "I need to go to the toilet," I said when she arrived, and she detached me from the IPC device and watched over me while I slowly and painfully swung round and dropped down from the bed. As soon as I was through the bathroom door, I knew I was going to be sick, but I stood in some confusion for a couple of seconds while the nurse suggested I get back into bed. Fortunately, instinct and common sense kicked in and I dropped to my knees in front of the toilet.

Such relief.

Back in bed, under the still smothering blankets and affixed to the relentlessly humming IPC machine, I couldn't get to sleep until about 2.15am – and woke at 5.15am needing the toilet again. Breakfast arrived about an hour later, swiftly followed by Mr A, who woke me from a doze with a big smile and reassurances that the operation had gone well.

"Got a nice lot of lymph nodes out. I had to cut a nerve, but…" and he shrugged, an action that halted any questions I might have had, since it implied normality, nothing to worry about. I would apparently be unhindered by permanent numbness in my inner upper arm.

The week following the operation was one of rest and recovery, but the horrific black and blue bruising and the pain as I stretched to remove mugs from the kitchen cupboard were nothing compared with the sheer hope and optimism that now suffused me. Only the radiotherapy to go now.

The end was a bright star guiding me.

I Aitken

The Grief

Uncle had been ill, with a disease called amyloidosis[65]: this caused a build-up of protein deposits in his vital organs. A late diagnosis meant aggressive treatment.

When I was about to start chemotherapy in the Spring, uncle called me. "It can be quite horrible," he said. "My nails fell off, and it can make you feel sick and tired. So if you need to chat, want to get things off your chest, just give me a call."

I really wish I had called him. At such a distance, I was unaware of just how ill he was. When he left the hospice and returned home, I thought it was because he was getting better, and would be fit enough to take care of himself. I don't know how I got it so wrong. Had my family been keeping the truth from me? Or had I just not been listening?

Uncle and aunt moved to Sussex from East London in 1979. My memories of their London home are almost non-existent, and those I do have are apparently wrong.

My memories of their Sussex cottage are much clearer, since they lived there throughout my childhood, and we frequently visited, exciting trips for a townie like me, since the wee cottage was perched on the edge of a wood, accessed via a long farm lane and then a footpath along the grassy borders of the trees.

The garden was usually populated by chickens, occasionally geese, and once – how exciting! – a baby kid goat.

Uncle was an occasional presence, returning from his work in construction in dusty trousers and muddy steel-capped boots. These latter were huge, as befitted the substantial, rugby-playing bear of a man that was my uncle. Much as I hate to surrender to such a cliché as "gentle giant", that's exactly what uncle was. He was big, and cuddly, with dark twinkly eyes framed by laughter lines, a slow drawl of a voice and a gentle humour. I didn't ever hear him shout.

The low ceilings of his 16th-century home forced a tall man to stoop – uncle had to stoop a lot. He was like Gulliver in Lilliput, except we Lilliputians didn't tie him down when he entered the house. He was a colossus in a doll's house, the compact dark rooms struggling to contain him. Yet, all the same, there was a deftness about him that meant he didn't, as you'd expect of a sizeable man, knock down ornaments or clatter off walls. His gentleness extended all around him, an aura, a shield.

Apart from on the rugby pitch, apparently, where he was tough enough to have almost made it into the England squad.

And this toughness was occasionally apparent in everyday life – having once been allowed to feed that kid goat milk from a bottle, the kid's fractious hunger forcing me into a tug-of-war battle, at our next visit I asked Uncle R where the absent baby goat was.

"In the freezer," said uncle, matter-of-factly, his stoicism more shocking to me than the thought of the goat in the freezer.

But uncle was among the most chilled out people I knew, always ready with a winking-eyed smile and a kind word for all those who sought his attention. His warmth and happy good nature worked well as the landlord of the pub uncle and aunt moved to; uncle holding court in the bar, filling pints and laughing with the locals. That move garnered me a lot of brownie points among my friends, who came with me to the annual music festival held in a marquee in the field next to the pub. They were amazing weekends of sunshine and cider, live music and laughter. Uncle would man the bar in the marquee, while my mum and dad helped behind the bar of the pub itself.

And then we lost him. I was devastated but, even more than that, so shocked. "I thought he was getting better!" I complained to mum down the phone. "He came home! He was getting better!" Her gentle contradiction of this belief allowed the stark truth to sink in. He didn't go home to get better. He went home to be with his loved ones.

And he had so many loved ones; not just his family, my cousins and their children, but also all the friends and acquaintances he made through the rugby club he was such an integral part of.

Eight days after my third and final operation, I made the 400-mile journey home to say goodbye to uncle. His funeral was held in the rugby club he helped to build, a party he should have been at, quite frankly. There was laughter at the anecdotes and at his nickname for my aunt, and also at the criminally short shorts he wore in the 70s; there was fond remembrance of his kindness, gentleness, humour, laughter and generosity.

That he is gone is fundamentally wrong.

He called me Smiler. He made me smile.

I Aitken

Chapter Fourteen

The private clinic did not have the capacity to offer radiotherapy, a treatment whose huge, expensive machines require radiation-proof building structures around them. I would be having this part of my treatment in the city's NHS hospital.

But first I met my radiotherapy consultant Dr P in the private clinic. (As I wracked my brains for the purpose of this book, I couldn't remember anything about where or when I might have met Dr P. This blurriness of memory is occurring more and more often, a lethal combination of mumnesia[66], chemo brain[67] and menopausal brain fog[68]. I recently incorrectly recalled that my radiotherapy had been once a week for a month, before suddenly remembering that in fact it had been daily for four weeks. The treatment is a haze of insanity and trauma. Much of the detail I can safely recollect is thanks to the blog I wrote, and the detailed calendar I kept. Any information that exists outwith those platforms is mired in amnesia. Fortunately, Dr P does appear briefly in the blog…)

She pointed out that she had the results of the third operation, but that she wasn't sure if she should share them with me, since I would be having an appointment with Mr A a couple of days later, when he would be telling me the results, and for Dr P to do so now would not only be a waste of everyone's time but would also steal Mr A's thunder. Dr P and I looked at each other.

"Mr A removed nine lymph nodes," she said, "none of which showed any sign of cancer." If the lymph nodes had been cancerous, chemotherapy would have destroyed the cancer cells but left scarring. So the micrometastases that had shown up on the first nodes Mr A removed were the the only cancer to have spread. It had gone no further before treatment. Yeah, I was pretty elated.

"So, because the cancer had not spread further among your axilla," said Dr P, "you'll only need radiotherapy on your breast, not further up your chest and neck. You'll receive treatment every weekday for four weeks…"

"Four weeks?" I interrupted. "I thought it would be three."

"Yes, four weeks, every day except weekends. It should be over by about Christmas." At this point, in a panic, I thought of all the celebratory events I had organised to mark when I thought would be the end of treatment: going to the cinema with son to see *Star Wars: The Last Jedi*; a family reunion and big lunch at a very posh hotel/restaurant; a spa weekend with husband; and the annual Christmas trip to the ballet with son and daughter. I didn't list all these to Dr P, feeling a bit foolish about my eagerness and ignorance.

"We'll make sure it's all done by Christmas," said Dr P, looking at my stricken face. (Remember her words. They are important.)

And then Dr P outlined the side effects of radiotherapy: cumulative tiredness; a sensation of burnt, reddened skin; possible scarring of the lung; increased weakening of the bones…

Truly? I didn't care. Whatever. By now I had accepted that side effects were a necessary evil, and quite frankly, having gone through chemo I thought radiotherapy would have to go some to prove itself more irritating. Bring it on.

So, two days after seeing Dr P, I was back to see Mr A, having promised that I wouldn't tell him that Dr P had already given me the results. "He'll be disappointed," Dr P had said. Unfortunately, in our attempt to protect Mr A's ego, I kind of landed Dr P in the doghouse. When Mr A revealed there had been no more signs of cancer, something I already knew, I, as promised, feigned surprise and delight. I felt the deceit burning my ears, but only really worried when Mr A said, "You saw Dr P a couple of days ago – what did you talk about?"

"Um, just about the radiotherapy treatment really," I lied, suddenly realising that I couldn't remember a single word of what we had talked about, other than the results that she wasn't supposed to talk about.

"She could have checked your scar, too," said Mr A. "I suppose as a practitioner she didn't think it was her job." The thing is, Dr P had checked my scar; and by failing to defend her, all I was doing was cementing whatever professional rivalry Mr A's comment signified.

I kept my mouth shut, though.

What I didn't keep my mouth shut about was the bloody excruciating "cording" I was now suffering in my right arm, thanks to the full axillary clearance. I had heard of this condition – officially called axillary web syndrome[69] – and because I'm an idiot not given it much credence, but as far as I was now concerned it had not been mentioned often enough or in strong enough terms.

It's flipping painful.

The only way I could think to describe it is in its similarity to tight hamstrings. If you, like me, struggle to touch your toes without bending your knees, you'll be aware of the stretching sensation in the backs of your thighs – cording feels like that but 100 times worse. It's caused by scar tissue, but it feels as though under your skin there's a rope that's too short for your arm; if you try to stretch your arm to its full length, it pulls with an agony that feels as though it will simply snap with a ping. Occasionally I was almost overwhelmed by the desire to grab a knife and slice through the roped tendons of my arm, just for the relief.

"Ah yes," said Mr A in answer to my whining. "We don't quite know why that happens but we think it's just an overreaction to surgical trauma."

Well, that would make sense. I had been a bit self-congratulatory about my rapid healing so far, my ability to recover quickly from surgery; but *over*reaction would be typical of me. My body's ability to heal itself had gone slightly too far and over-healed.

"You've done very well through all this," said Mr A. "You've coped well. It's not usual to have two axillary biopsies. It's been hard work for you."

I blinked. Chemo nurse MO had said I made it look easy, and now Mr A said it had been hard work. And wait – it wasn't usual to have two axillary biopsies? How was I supposed to know that? It's all very well for all these medical experts to have the bigger picture, to watch thousands of patients come through the process every year, but it was my first time. They seemed to be pinning me up on a league table of how patients respond to treatment; I was *here* on the Y axis of patients who'd had two axillary clearances but *here* on the X axis of having made it all look easy. (See *plate ii*).

But I had no league tables and no other frames of reference. I turned up as an amateur, and literally did as I was told. If I had known that having more than one axilla clearance was unusual, I might have been a bit more worried. If I had thrown up after every meal during chemotherapy, I might have struggled more to cope. As it was, my story was my story; my experience was my experience. I could only react to my environment as befitted my character.

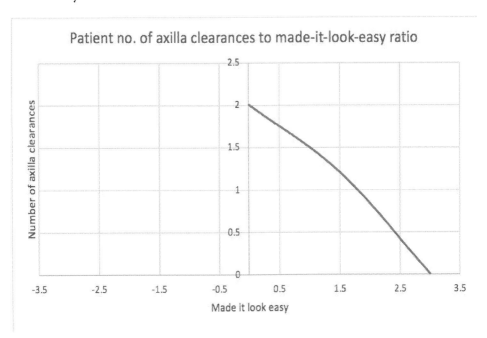

Plate ii

I don't know why I've fixated so much on that point.

Back to the cording, which apparently would be curable, though I didn't see how. It seemed a part of me now. But after two absolutely agonising sessions of physio – during which the scarring was broken up with firm massaging and rubbing up my arm – I achieved greater movement and flexibility. The exercises I was given I practised with masochistic pleasure, hoping that just one stretch would see the scar tissue sever and, with a pop, release the tension.

The pain didn't stop me having one of the best birthday weekends ever.

I mean, I've had some pretty incredible birthdays, along with some very unmemorable ones, though I forget those, but this year's was, for obvious reasons, rather special. Husband, kids and I went to see *Paddington 2* at the cinema; we settled down with a takeaway in front of Friday night telly; I stayed in bed all the next day eating chocolate; and husband took me out for a meal, with good friends also joining us as a surprise. (Husband managed the most amazing surprises for my 40th birthday, involving a spa treatment, birthday party and weekend trip to Paris, so now reckons himself something of a birthday surprise guru.)

It was a weekend I needed, surrounded by family and friends, a weekend of normality. I was so unbelievably, quietly happy.

Before I began the radiotherapy, I needed to undergo the measurements and planning session, which I used to complete a reconnaissance trip to the hospital in town. I would be getting there by train and bus for the four weeks of treatment, so I decided to travel that way for this appointment, to learn the route.

The journey was rapid, smooth and simple. Sitting on the top deck of the bus as it navigated through the city was actually a pleasure – I felt as though I was on holiday.

Once at hospital, I waited only a little while before being taken through to the CT scanner.

I removed my top clothes behind a curtain, and draped what amounted to a tiny paper hand towel over my chest before rejoining the nurses at the CT scanner. I was carefully positioned on the bed with my arms above my head, and told to maintain this posture. "Is it uncomfortable?" asked one of the nurses, and since the cording in my right arm was stretching to the point of agony, yes, it was sodding uncomfortable.

"It's fine," I said through gritted teeth.

The nurses murmured to one another, drawing straight lines across my torso with a red pen; and then they were gone, leaving me alone in the cold room while they operated the scanner. The scanner started up its aeroplane engine hum, and I lay absolutely still as the bed slid me in and out the CT machine.

When the scan was finished, the nurses returned. "We need to make a small tattoo[70] on your chest as a marker for the radiotherapy," said the nurse. "Is that okay? It's a very tiny dot. You can hardly see it."

I was fine with this, since I already had a tattoo. And that was not, of course, a mere dot. But what did they do, I wondered, about those who did refuse a tattoo? Had anyone ever refused the tattoo? (Another quick online search divulges the fact that some women are actually bothered by the idea of a tattoo, which I suspect is more to do with the permanence of such a mark. It's actually such a minuscule dot, it's not noticeable at all, apart from for the nurses doing the radio treatment. The alternative is to use marker pen, but since this can eventually wear and wash off, it wouldn't guarantee a thoroughly precise treatment of the cancer area. Get me – medical expert.)

A couple of quick, almost entirely painless needle pricks into the skin, and I was invited to get dressed and leave. A ten-minute session, after a 45-minute journey into hospital. This was a mere taster for things to come.

All thoughts of radiotherapy thrust aside, I continued my determined return to normal life with a trip to the theatre to see *Trainspotting*. The actor playing Renton was the son of an acquaintance of mine; what tickled me was that this drug-addled, heroin-deranged failure of a human was being played by the son of a pastor. It was a couple of hours of the most intense and visceral entertainment, at once comical and pathetic – a useful reminder of the city's drug hell past. Watching a heroin addict dive into a toilet in his smack-headed hallucinations – the best way to forget about one's own concerns.

And just to make sure that I didn't remain too self-absorbed, husband managed to seriously injure his ankle while playing volleyball, thus reaffirming what we already knew – that I would make a terrible nurse. When he returned early from the sports centre, I lay in bed listening to him hopping heavily along the hall, and my heart sank. Sure enough, he lumbered up the stairs and launched himself onto the bed, groaning and repeatedly saying, "I'm so annoyed." Before he could even explain what the problem was – though the ice pack taped round his ankle was a fair sign – my immediate reaction was to think, *tell it to someone who gives a shit*. I didn't say that out loud because though I am possibly the most selfish person on the planet, I do have some idea of right and wrong. So I kept all thoughts of annoyance, and any frustration that my family would dare to become ill and injured while I had bloody cancer, to myself.

Husband's injury turned out to be a rather nasty sprain, and I felt sufficiently guilty about not giving him enough sympathy to bring him a couple of cups of tea in bed the following week.

And then, just as suddenly as it had appeared, the cording in my arm was gone. Not that I resented Mr A knowing more than I did about the condition, and not that I found his confident prognosis for it irritatingly blasé, but I was reminded of the feeling of not being in charge of my own body – of other (albeit professional) people having more knowledge and control.

I Aitken

The Objectification

The question of bodily autonomy arose several times during the nine months of cancer treatment, and it reminded me of a few times when I felt that my body was suddenly no longer my own – that other people had, or were trying to, sequestrate it.

On one particularly humiliating occasion, a personal trainer in my London gym decided to lie on top of me on the exercise ball, in a hall separate from everybody else.

I was going through one of my occasional fitness phases, and had booked this particular bloke to motivate me over about six sessions, I think it was. He was obviously his number one fan. I forget what pretence it was under that he took me out of the packed gym and into this separate hall – maybe something to do with loosening and stretching my back muscles. He claimed the best way to do this was for me to lie on top of the ball, rolling gently backwards and forwards. So far, so harmless. Then, with no warning or question of consent, he lay on top of me. I was smothered by his weight, and my shock, discomfort and embarrassment. There was a wall of mirrors that I consciously avoided looking at. I couldn't bear the thought of what I must look like in this undignified position.

I'm still not convinced that this was the best way to stretch my back muscles.

A couple of times over the years I have gone along to my GP, whoever that is wherever I live at the time, and requested a health check – a sort of MOT. They never seem surprised at my request, or unwilling to carry it out as a waste of resources; but I have to confess that the reason I've had it done was mainly through a fear that I was living too hard and maybe not taking enough care of myself. I get liver and kidney function, and blood sugar level tests, a BMI check, cholesterol check, etc, and it's always come back tip-top tickety boo.

One I had in London, however, was not such a tickety boo experience. I was 31. I had just started dating husband. I decided to get myself all checked out and serviced, as it were, and also enquire as to the reason for my sore breasts, which had been feeling bruised on and off for a short while.

The GP I saw was an elderly gent. I had never met him before. I wasn't a frequent visitor to the doctor in those days.

I explained why I was there, and he said, "You look perfectly fit to me." I bristled immediately. I did not like his tone.

"Oh, I'm terribly unfit,' I said. "I tried going running with my boyfriend and it almost killed me."

"Well, regular sex is good for fitness, so I'm sure you're very fit…" said the GP, and he winked at me.

He winked at me.

I genuinely didn't know what to say to this. It was all wrong. He was a doctor, someone I should be able to trust implicitly, someone who should be sexless and neutral and not bloody embarrassing. I thought if I said nothing and maintained a completely blank face, the comment would evaporate and never have existed.

I explained why I was there, and also broached the subject of my tender boobs.

"Pull up your shirt and undo your bra," he said.

I have to confess I rather thought that he would have left the room to fetch a female nurse as chaperone. But he didn't. And I didn't say anything. And I did as I was told.

I stood topless before him, and he grasped my breasts in his hands, gently squeezing them and prodding my neck. Then he leant forward and said,

"You have very beautiful breasts."

At this point my sense of self returned and I retorted, "I'm not sure you should speak to me like that." He began stammering and stepped quickly away, motioning for me to get dressed. The tone shifted entirely, and he retreated back into a clinical distance as he asked me to step on the scales.

(See, now this is interesting. This reminds me of the embarrassing scene

I enforced on the ultrasound doctor. It was okay for me to make that doctor feel awkward, but absolutely not okay for this London doctor to make me feel awkward. I'll explain why. It's to do with the balance of power and punching above your weight. The London doctor held the power; I trusted him. From his position, his behaviour was intimidating. And Dr C the ultrasound guy was also the figure of authority and held the power, and I was in a vulnerable and self-conscious position, so I used the subject of sex – which is personal and intimate – to undermine his intimidating position. Making him feel as awkward as I did, lying there on a bed in a darkened room with no top on, balanced the power. That was the self-confidence that comes with age and experience.)

But I was mistaken in thinking I had put the London GP in his place. He explained that the bruised sensation in my breast tissue was probably due to the Pill, and that I should welcome any breast growth because it would get me lots of male attention.

God, it's so weird the thoughts and sensations you go through when in this position. I am nothing if not bolshy and defensive. How the hell I didn't completely lose my shit at this I still have no idea. Something to do with the sense that he was a person of authority, an expert, I was in a safe place… I felt myself shut down, and decided that the only way I could defend myself and get through this appointment was to laugh it all off.

Oh, ha ha ha! How amusing you are, belittling my health concerns and reducing me to a mere plaything for men! Hee hee hee!

He agreed to take some bloods for testing, and so I rolled up my sleeve. Once he had drawn the blood, however, he said,

"Oh, I don't have any cotton wool. Could you just hold the needle there a second?" I obediently took gentle hold of the needle, which was still sticking out my arm, unfazed but also very aware that this was hardly professional behaviour on his part, while he scooted across the room on his chair and rifled through some boxes on the shelf for cotton wool.

Once the needle was removed, pressure applied, and a plaster placed over the tiny puncture, the appointment ended with the GP telling me I had nothing to worry about. I left.

I felt sick. I felt revolted. I drove to work. I worked with mostly men and when I arrived in the office I explained the experience I had just gone through. They were horrified.

But I never reported the doctor, and I never saw him again. When I went back for the blood test results I made sure I saw a different GP. What sort of response was that old man expecting? If I hadn't finally – finally! – told him to stop, how else did he think I was going to take it? Did he want to make me feel uncomfortable? Or flattered? Or attractive? Or intimidated?

What I did feel was unclean, for several weeks afterwards. Unclean and at fault.

When I gave birth to my daughter, child number two (so I knew what to expect and how to do it, as it were), I failed to deliver the placenta. Oh! Ha! Look at that – a language of failure, like it was my fault the placenta wouldn't eject, like I wasn't trying hard enough. I pushed, I genuinely did. But there were no more contractions now the baby was out – I didn't know how to engage the necessary muscles.

So down to theatre I went to have the placenta removed manually. I can honestly place that up there with one of the most humiliating, unpleasant experiences I have ever endured, and I've farted during sex.

For a start I was shocked by the number of people in theatre – my memory is hazy but I have an idea there were about six. My next shock was the fact that one of the surgical staff was a man. For the births of both my children, I had specified I wanted only female midwives, no students and my husband the only man in that room where my nether regions were to be split asunder.

"Oh," I giggled nervously, "You're a man!"

"Last time I looked," he said. Suck it up, was the message then. I was a procedure, with no choice.

It took some time to benumb my lower half. The initial local anaesthetic wouldn't take at all, and I spent some time just sitting on the bed waiting for something to happen. I threw up at one point. It was all very unpleasant. Eventually I was given an epidural, which worked almost immediately, and I was laid down. And then I saw a foot up by my cheek.

"Whose foot is that?" I asked.

"It's yours," said a nurse, gently. I felt sick and dizzy. My feet have never been up by my cheek, that's not where they belong and it shouldn't be physically possible.

"I think I'm going to faint," I said. The nurse understandingly coaxed me into conversation, knowing that, by talking, my breath would be regulated and the dizziness would pass.

I can't remember how long the whole procedure took. A couple of hours, I think, but when someone has their hand thrust far up into your body, fishing in your uterus for a meaty mass, you tend to drift off and pretend it's not happening.

And then the hand and placenta were removed, with one of the most deadening, patronising, humiliating statements the registrar could deliver: "That was easy."

The placenta had apparently come away from the wall of my uterus with ease and little manipulation on her part. And with that statement came the implication that if only I had pushed just a little bit harder on the labour ward, I could have expelled it myself with none of this nonsense, and without wasting everyone's time. I had lost control of my own body and somehow it was my fault. It was very odd, at 36 and as the mother of two children, to be made to feel like a fractious teenager.

I Aitken

Chapter Fifteen

espite all I had already gone through, I was desperately nervous about my first radiotherapy[71] session. I felt ridiculous, and vaguely annoyed. Bloody three operations and a course of chemotherapy down the line, and I was still anxious about the easiest part of the treatment.

The night before my first session, I complained I was feeling cold, and had a wee dram of brandy to warm myself up. I mean, I didn't honestly think that brandy could do for me what a blanket, heater and hot water bottle weren't already. Of course not. Though I was maybe trying to fool husband, I couldn't fool myself. That brandy was a little shot of Dutch courage.

And boy, was I glad I had already completed a reconnaissance mission for the CT planning scan. It meant I knew which bus stop to head for out of the train station, and which buses I could jump on, without getting stressed or wasting time looking them up on my phone, while standing in the torrent of commuters and tourists on the pavement. Still, it was definitely an adventure. So much of the previous eight months of treatment had been about staying at home, I was heartily sick of my bed and the sofa, and it was a joy to be out on my own, in the buzz of the city.

A minor hiccup when I arrived at hospital – I wasn't entirely sure where I needed to be. It wasn't in the waiting room for the previous CT planning session, that much I did know. I wandered around a bit, glancing at a number of what seemed to be reception desks, all with thoroughly absorbed nurses standing at them. Eventually I interrupted a quiet conversation between several healthcare professionals in front of a computer screen, and asked them where I needed to be. Linac 6 apparently, so I headed for the tiny waiting area assigned to such a machine.

Four or five pairs of eyes stared at me as I navigated ankles to sit down. "Good morning!" I called cheerfully, in an attempt to thaw the baltic atmosphere.

"Morning," came the muted reply.

I braved the silence for a full second before saying, "Well, this is a quiet party, isn't it?" Usually my gobbiness gets people's backs up but fortunately this audience was a lighthearted one, so the comment proved an ice breaker.

A note on my fellow radiotherapy patients:

The hospital was host to seven radiotherapy Linac machines (Linac being short for linear accelerator). Each machine had its designated, small waiting area. In most cases, patients are assigned the same Linac for all their treatments (apart from the final couple of sessions, which are on a super speedy machine). This means that you are seeing the same patients every day for some time, facilitating short-lived but warm-hearted acquaintanceships.

That first day in the waiting area, I wasn't sure who were the patients and who were the spouses/partners – this obviously became clear as each person was called up for their treatment. Those who had been there often already were engaging with one another and having a laugh, especially one or two particular characters, who had a barbed sense of humour and took no prisoners.

One announced that her 35-year-old twins would be visiting for Christmas. "And my son has decided he's a vegan, so I have no idea what to do. You can't make a turkey out of tofu."

"And vegan cheese is disgusting," said the other woman. "You could tie your plants up with it."

"They'd withstand a gale," agreed woman one.

During the four weeks that I spent commuting into the city for this treatment, these fellow patients made it all the more bearable. They were the briefest of friendships, but they were relationships forged by a shared experience.

Where I had been one of the lucky ones in the chemo suite, experiencing little sickness and having a positive prognosis, here too I was aware of how lucky I was. One woman, whose wheelchair was manoeuvred carefully by her husband, had had repeated cancers and treatments for the past 17 years but remained gently and sweetly smiling. She told me her story with so little self-pity, I was humbled.

"I don't know how you've come through all of this," I said.

"Well, you just do, don't you?" she replied. "I have my down days, of course I do, I'm only human; but then you pick yourself up, dust yourself down, and get on with it. Although in my case," she pointed at her wheelchair, "not very fast."

And then there was the gent whose own wheelchair was parked in the corridor by a porter. I asked if he would like to turn round and join the rest of us. During the next couple of days, I learned that he was receiving palliative care – as he stumbled through his own story, emphasising the parts that perplexed him and skimming through the parts he didn't understand so well, I suddenly realised that his palliative treatment wasn't a cure. That he had nearly reached the end of his journey. I didn't see him again after that.

"The nurse'll be coming to get you in a minute," one patient said to me in a troublingly warning tone. "She'll give you a green plastic bag and a bottle of horrid-smelling moisturiser."

"Oh, god, that cream is grim," exclaimed another. "It smells so bad." A heated discussion began, with recommendations for alternative moisturisers. When a nurse arrived and called my name, sure enough she was bearing a green bag – there were cackles from the other patients.

The nurse led me into a small room, where she explained the process I was about to undergo, and the side effects[72] I might experience: sore skin, tiredness, difficulties swallowing... She produced a bottle of the "horrid-smelling" moisturiser, and advised that I should smear it liberally on the part of my chest that would be exposed to the radiation therapy.

"Your skin can go a bit red, as though you've been sun burnt," she said.

In my eagerness to be at the hospital in time for this first treatment session, I had arrived an hour early. This meant I had an hour in which to absorb the stories, jollity and distractions of the other patients in the waiting area. This, for a time, meant my irritating anxieties had been suppressed. But suppressed anxieties do not stay suppressed for ever. Eventually, they find their way to the surface. As I was led into the treatment room for the first time, I could feel a cold sweat gently breaking out – the first sign I was gearing up for a proper old anxiety attack, such as I had not experienced for some years.

In that state, I failed to take in my surroundings in any detail. All I was aware of was a large, cold, clinical room, with a bed in the middle, around which three or four nurses were standing chatting. They turned to smile at me as I was brought in by one of their colleagues. I was shepherded into a small changing cubicle, where I removed my upper clothes, and again covered my top with a paper towel, aka a modesty sheet. What the point of that was I've no idea, since as soon as I was laid down on the bed the sheet was removed and my boobs were laid bare. It's almost as though when you're lying down on the hospital bed you're a number, a case; but standing up and talking you're suddenly a person with an identity, a character – you are a naked human.

Anyway, lying on the bed, with the modesty sheet removed and my arms above my head, the nurses stood looking over me, talking quietly to each other, repeating and checking numbers. A red laser light beamed down on me from the ceiling, and little red crosses were drawn with pen at the points where the tattoos had been made.

Before the nurses withdrew from the room, one told me, "This first session will be slightly longer than the rest, because we'll be using the x-ray panels to make sure all the measurements are correct. We don't use the x-rays in every session. The panels will be moving all around you, so just stay absolutely still. We'll be out in the corridor but we can see you, so if you have any problems, just raise a hand." And they left.

The machinery started its gentle humming very shortly afterwards, but in that brief gap was an experiential limbo, a silence and space which, far from being restful, only allowed my subconscious to string together hundreds of frightened thoughts. But they were subconscious, so I wasn't really aware of them. My conscious merely told me to lie still and wait. Silly conscious. Silly, naive conscious.

The x-ray panels of the Linac machine slid up beside my body; I was very aware of them in my peripheral vision. I could have kept my eyes closed – I discovered many other patients did so – but I found this impossible. With the humming and the whirring and the movement of a machine around me, it was too unnerving not to know what was going on.

I found myself staring into what I could only describe as the face of the machine. A large glass screen which covered I knew not what – a lens? A laser? – hovered above me. I was overwhelmed by the sense that I was being watched, and not just by the nurses out in the corridor. I stared at the machine with fascination, running my eye over all the intricate parts within view, wondering how it worked; and bubbling beneath this fascination was a growing fear. My powerful subconscious dread thrust aside any conscious logic and launched itself into an anxiety attack.

I have had many anxiety attacks in my life. I know the signs and symptoms. Fortunately, I have also been given the tools to control them to a large extent. As my breathing shallowed, my skin began to tingle and I felt my temperature rise. I made a conscious effort to control my breathing: *breathe in for four and out for six*, I thought. *I'll count to 600.* Such a small thing as controlling your breathing dissipates all the symptoms of panicking. You stop releasing adrenaline, you are inhaling and expelling the right quantities of oxygen… As a therapist once told me, you are not being chased by a tiger. It is occasionally necessary to remind myself of this fact, as a critical stumbling block for the fight or flight syndrome. What is there to fight? Nothing. What is there to flee? Nothing. So pull yourself together and breathe properly. It is all within your capabilities…

Racy narratives such as the above are what go through my mind as I take control of my primal instincts.

And I only made it to 450 before the nurses returned to my side, inviting me to sit up. Only 10 minutes were spent lying so still. Ten minutes, compared to the 45 or so it had taken me to get to the hospital and the hour I had spent waiting. That it was such an easy process I almost ruined with my angst annoyed me.

When I got home that evening, the emotion rose unchecked, manifesting itself in a variety of psychosomatic side effects. I was hit by an unusually strong bout of IBS and felt properly sick.

From then on I knew what was coming, and none of the next 18 sessions filled me with anything like the same anxiety. In fact, several times I forgot where I was, the machine humming around me as I lay still, silently planning for Christmas: what gifts I needed to buy for whom; what groceries to get in and when.

It was, however, several days before I took any proper notice of the Linac machine. I had been merrily waltzing in, removing my top, and lying down on the bed, without a second glance at the contraption standing at the head of the bed. This was, in part, because of the very clinical feel of the room. The whole process I found to be like a factory conveyor belt: there were so many radio patients, we were fed through the system one after another, like rats in a lab, stripped, laid down, blasted, dressed, and sent on our way. Despite the polite pleasantries proffered by the nurses, there was little warmth or humanity about the procedure.

This meant that I, like the lab rat being guided through the system, obediently stripped, laid down, was blasted, then dressed and went on my way, with little attention paid to the wider view.

But one day, I left the changing cubicle and just seemed to open my mind and vision to this huge contraption.

"Wow!" I exclaimed. "It's actually massive, isn't it?" I had only ever been staring into the "collimator" – the part that delivers the radiation beam. But of course it required a much larger machine – the "gantry" – to deliver this beam.

One of the radiation therapists explained the process.

"The machine accelerates electrons, and then they produce high-energy x-rays [having collided with a metal target]. The x-rays are shaped to your cancer, and then the beam is directed straight to it."

There is a lot of humming while the process occurs, but I knew when I was being blasted by the invisible x-ray beam because a continuous 30-second beep was emitted. Every day I would spend roughly five minutes on the bed, during which I was hit by three 30-second beeps. Those cold, topless five minutes were a minor inconvenience in my exciting daily excursion into the city.

On day three, the machinery failed to start its regulation humming after the nurses had left the room. One returned to let me know that the computer had crashed, and was I okay to just stay in this position? I said yes.

Yes to lying on my back, cold and topless, with my arms above my head, like some sort of horizontal porn cheerleader. I was locked into this position for 20 minutes, but eventually I couldn't move anyway, thanks to the air conditioning.

But I didn't bat an eyelid. I couldn't, they were frozen stiff.

I Aitken

The Emotional Impact

So what impact did all this have on my family? Overtly, it was barely noticeable. But in actuality it was enormous. No-one should underestimate the burden that is carried by a cancer patient's friends and family. It is a long drawn-out process, of illness and treatment, tears, regrets and fears.

"I don't know how you're coping with all this," I said to husband midway through the year. He not only had to continue working, but also ferry me to all my operations and chemo sessions, support me, feed me, make sure the children were fed and dressed, and where they should be at any given time… Basically perform the duties of two parents, while also caring for a sick wife.

"I just take each day as it comes," he said pragmatically. (I shall come back to this.)

And since the illness itself had had little conspicuous impact on me, the children were blissfully unaware that anything was wrong until I started having treatment.

That's not quite true.

After my diagnosis in Tokyo's St Luke's International Hospital, as we descended the escalator from the Breast Cancer department, I immediately told the children about my illness. And son immediately burst into tears. I had forgotten that two teachers at his school had recently died of different forms of cancer, so naturally he readily associated cancer with death.

(This reflects the general stigma around "the C word" – people are still known to whisper it, or avoid it entirely. This despite the fact that there are a myriad different cancers, few of which are the fault of their sufferers, and most of which can now be treated and/or cured. I don't understand this extreme reticence. Nobody seems to whisper pneumonia, which can be just as devastating; or syphilis, whose infection is usually due to sheer carelessness and therefore much more embarrassing.)

We reassured son and persuaded him I would not die. After that, there was no obvious reason for him and his sister to worry. Until after the first operation, when I was suddenly clearly vulnerable, and the children were led into my bedroom when they came home from school to give me a gentle kiss and hug. Then daughter especially was woken to the fact of my illness; the next day, I felt good enough to get up and have a shower, where I was accompanied by daughter, who repeatedly asked if I was okay, and watched with captivated curiosity as I slowly and carefully dried myself. Since I couldn't bend over to pull up my hold-ups, she helped me, then started chanting, "Will the cancer go? Will it ever go?" I looked at her with some consternation, but found her staring at her reflection in the mirror, watching the crocodile tear she had forced out rolling down her cheek.

At not quite seven years of age, she had apparently caught on to the fact that perhaps my illness was something she should be worried about, something that should affect her. In reality, she was more fascinated than frightened.

Actually, daughter's response was more complex than that. Consciously, she didn't understand what she needed to be worried about; which, subconsciously, meant she was very worried, but she didn't know that, and she didn't know why. Bit of cod child psychology there. It was very rare for daughter to have tantrums but one day in the summer, as I took her to tennis camp, we found out that the young lad she was supposed to be having a playdate with that afternoon was ill, so she wouldn't be able to go to his house after all. Daughter, surprisingly, was inconsolable. The poor lad's illness was apparently not good enough a reason to postpone their date. She cried, and I felt helpless, and when I told her she could play with him some other day, she squeaked her disapproval of this plan. It wasn't good enough, apparently. I was taken aback by her reaction, and felt genuinely helpless.

And then another mum, who I didn't know at all but whose daughter was in my daughter's year at school, suggested we all have a picnic together the next day after tennis. Daughter's sobs subsided. I learnt two things in that instant: that daughter was, after all, affected by my illness; and that people can be surprisingly kind.

And then daughter developed an alarming facial tic, regularly blinking hard and screwing up her nose. Every night she complained of having a sore stomach, and I knew that these must be psychosomatic[73] symptoms of her unease. Though the facial tic disappeared as quickly as it arrived, she still, to this day (the day I'm writing. Sunday), suffers inexplicable tummy aches.

And, of course, she had no idea why she was displaying such symptoms of anxiety and no conscious understanding of why she should worry about my illness. A seven-year-old has little empathy. Well, my seven-year-old.

Midway through chemo, when I moved from the first round of violent drugs onto the less abusive Taxol, I set off for the High Street accompanied by daughter, a journey I hadn't made for some time, and one that I was nervous about, picturing myself overheating and fainting with the overexertion.

"If I need to sit down, or feel funny, I'll need you to be a big girl and get me some help, okay?" I said to daughter. She looked at me in complete incomprehension. It was a look I couldn't fully interpret. Did she think that since I was on my feet there was no cause for concern and I should just get on with it? Or did she think, *I'm seven. What the heck can I do? That's just too much responsibility for you to burden me with.*

As it happened, I had absolutely no problem with the walk, and had hugely underestimated how strong and fit I was.

"You're walking as fast as I am, mummy," said daughter admiringly and slightly patronisingly. I had given her cause for concern, yet here I was coping perfectly well. I was a fraud.

Son's reaction to my illness was much more subtle. There were no psychosomatic symptoms, and no overt neuroses. After that first tearful response to my diagnosis he wended his way through his wee life, accepting every event in my treatment, questioning nothing.

The first sign I had that he had been more affected than I realised was the following year, when I was ostensibly all better.

Treatment was finished. I was "cured". We had embarked on a year of living life to the full, clawing back the time we had lost to cancer.

We were in the USA for a couple of weeks, travelling from San Francisco to Seattle to Vancouver. During a bike ride over the Golden Gate bridge, son had something of a pre-pubescent tantrum. I can't remember what it was about; it was unimportant. But I remember saying to him, "I just want us all to have a lovely time together as a family, because last year was so rubbish."

And son replied, quick as a whip, "That was last year. You're better now." The inference was twofold: 1) I no longer had cancer so I should get over it and stop using it as an emotional weapon; and/or 2) I no longer had cancer and he didn't want to be reminded of it. That is, it was in the past, and that's where he would like it to stay.

And I was suffused with such a complexity of emotions at this: embarrassment at the idea he would think I was using my illness as emotional blackmail; and a sudden huge realisation that my son had been affected after all, that he wasn't immune to the stress and worry, that we hadn't paid him sufficient attention or given him enough reassurance.

As for husband's pragmatism… It is all well and good to take each day as it comes, to cross a bridge only when you arrive at it. I wouldn't presume to analyse husband, but I will say that I don't believe for one moment that it is possible to work, to look after children, to tend to a sick partner, to take on so many financial, emotional and practical duties, without it having a massive mental and emotional impact.

Cancer is not a cold. Though, in many cases, it is curable, its poisonous tentacles wrap themselves around both patient and loved ones, scalding and scarring and forever leaving a mark.

Chapter Sixteen

T hanks to an uncertainty around precise treatment dates, a slight breakdown in communication and a massive bout of optimism on my part, I was under the misconception that all my treatment would be over by the beginning of December.

It wasn't.

But I had booked a string of events to celebrate getting my life back, and there wasn't the slightest chance that any of these would be postponed or cancelled.

First up was my family – mum and dad, brother, sister-in-law, nephew and niece – travelling 400 miles to join us in a slap-up expensive meal at a local, very posh restaurant. This restaurant is so posh and expensive, it can only be visited when we have something super special to celebrate, like a Nobel prize win or something. I thought that being cured of cancer was up there among such occasions worthy of expensive celebration. So family duly arrived for a couple of nights.

Incidentally, I had also arranged for a local photographer to come to the house and take nice shots of son and daughter, for reasons that are too boring even for me to go into.

Photographer arrived, and clocked the rest of my family. "Would you like me to take shots of you all?" she asked kindly. And when dad told her of the reason they were all visiting, she was even more insistent on spending even more of her surely valuable Saturday taking pictures of my family. The photo session turned into an event in its own right, with various members of the family taking turns to be shot with one another. It was extremely exciting.

And then we all set off for posh restaurant, and had the most spanking, swanky meal imaginable, with nary an eyelid batted by the waiting staff at my blue wig, which I took off halfway through the lunch thanks to heat and itchiness.

Celebratory event number one out the way.

A couple of days later I was at the physio for lymphoedema[74] treatment, which can consist only of a gentle massaging around the lymph glands of the neck and chest, encouraging drainage elsewhere in the body of the fluids that build up in the arm, thanks, in my case, to the removal of all lymph glands in my right armpit. This was a side effect I hadn't been prepared for. Forsaking treatment can result in a very swollen hand, whose skin is smooth and tight with the engorged fluids within. Even minor scratches are more prone to become infected, thanks to the limited flow of white blood cells to the area, so it's important to protect the skin on lymphoedema-affected limbs.

And still the radiotherapy continued, my journey into the city hospital every morning, by train and bus, regular enough that I began to see the same people and strike up conversations with them. The lovely Pauletta – I shall call her Pauletta though that isn't her name – was my most amusing companion. She was regularly travelling into the city for Christmas shopping, but where she would travel by train, her husband insisted on getting the bus, and they would meet somewhere in town. I found this sweetly eccentric.

When *Star Wars: The Last Jedi* was launched in cinemas, I made sure to buy tickets for me and son to see it on the first night. This, for some reason I have never been able to pin down, meant we ended up at a cinema in the far west of the city. Husband was concerned.

"Be careful," he said. "Where's the cinema?"

"It's right next to the train station, so you don't have to worry. In fact, I've been there before! You remember, to see the fracking film," I was touched, bemused and amused by his concern.

Husband seemed unpersuaded.

"Is it a dodgy part of town?" I asked.

"Yes," he said.

"We'll be fine," I said.

I drove me and son to the cinema. It was fine. And it was a film suitably dramatic for my state of mind, because I love *Star Wars*.

The next day, the linear accelerator I received my treatment on was broken – it often was – and I was sent home untreated, but with the casual remark that I would receive two treatment sessions in one day the next week.

That weekend, husband and I took a well-earned break to a spa hotel in the Scottish borders. Husband had never had a spa break or massage before, and I told him he was in for a treat. A snowfall in the hills meant that we were lucky to even arrive at the hotel – at one point, with husband doing wheel spins up a steep hill and a valley drop behind us, I thought we might have to spend the weekend in a local farmhouse instead.

The hotel, of course, was lovely. After the 10 months we had been through, it was strangely romantic, being able to spend this time together without it involving operations or needles and drugs.

When husband returned from his first massage of the day (he had booked two), I asked him how it had gone, expecting him to melt with bliss before my eyes.

"It was okay," he said. "But I felt a bit sick and faint at one point. I told the masseuse and she said that was normal, and she paused for a bit. And then later on my nose and lips went numb but she said she'd never heard of that happening before."

My husband is unique.

He delayed his second treatment while he recovered from the first.

The weekend was a success – the snow made the view from our window fairytale magical. It felt as though Christmas was truly on its way, a beautiful end to a godawful year. And I am now convinced that massages and spa treatments should be available on the NHS for cancer patients, or anyone with a long-term health problem. It's a release, a total relaxation, a period of utter blankness, of being pampered and literally thoughtless. (And oo look! A quick bit of research shows that massage is indeed offered as part of cancer care in some health centres[75]! Not mine, though. Sad face.)

And then it was the final week of treatment. By now, all extra-curricular activities aside, I was pretty damn tired. And so I should have been. While radiotherapy treatment is, ostensibly, a doddle, the work it actually does on the body is understandably draining. It takes up far more of one's energy than one realises.

So, each day of treatment, you are blasted by radiotherapy x-rays, which finally destroy any and every cancer cell that has managed to slip through the chemo; and, of course, such a process also damages, to some extent, the surrounding healthy cells and tissue. At which point, when that five-minute blast of radiation is finished, the body goes into overdrive, mending and replacing all the damaged healthy cells, and cleaning up the destroyed cancer cells[77]. It's a ruddy marvel of a process, and one which, every single day, uses up so much of the body's energy, without you even realising or feeling it.

Anyway, the Monday of the final treatment week I turned up and was told by a nurse that since I had missed the previous Friday's treatment, I would have my final session tacked onto the end, on the 27th December.

"No, I won't," I said. The nurse assumed a poker face. "I can have two sessions in one day, can't I? I've heard that's possible. I'd rather do that."

"Well, yes, it might be possible, but I think the doctor would rather you had another session right at the end. It's very tiring having two in one day." Like a toddler refusing to let go of a lollypop, I was adamant. "I had been told that all my treatment would be over by Christmas, so I've got that into my head now. It's hard, you know, psychologically, to get past that deadline."

The nurse nodded sympathetically, and said she would speak to the doctor. I had my Monday session and returned home.

That afternoon the nurse called me.

"The doctors would still prefer it if you came in on the 27th but if you absolutely won't do that, you can have two sessions tomorrow," she said. "But there has to be as much time as possible between the treatments, so you'll need to come in at 8.45am for the first treatment, then 4.30pm for the second one."

If they thought that this "inconvenience" was going to change my mind, they were sorely mistaken.

"That would be perfect, thank you very much," I said.

I was strung to a tautness so physical I was practically a tennis racquet. This process was nearly over. I could so very nearly touch the finish line. Nothing – nothing – would interfere with that last day, its date carved on a monolith in my mind.

The following day, sure enough, I travelled twice into the city, making the train and bus journey both times. I didn't feel any more tired, receiving two sessions in one day – by this stage I was at peak exhaustion anyway. I was being kept alert and upright by adrenalin and excitement.

And then Friday 22nd December was upon us. The last day. I put my glad rags on and dolled up my face. After treatment I would head back into town to meet husband and children for lunch, from where I would take children to see the Scottish Ballet.

The journey into town was so familiar it felt like a daily commute; except that I was lugging a bag full of cakes and chocolates for the nurses, which made me feel more like Santa. When I arrived at the hospital, I offloaded the bag of sweets at the radio reception, noticing another two bags from other patients. I should imagine the nurses would have been so over chocolate by the end of Christmas.

The last few radiotherapy treatments were on a separate machine, a final, even faster blast, so I sat in the main waiting room, which meant there were no familiar faces, none of my fellow Linac 6 users. My insides were fizzing; I was a sherbet dip dab. And no-one else in this waiting room knew, or understood. I wanted a party. I wanted balloons. I got clinical smells, medical lino, and a solemn clutch of patients perched on chairs around me.

"You're looking glamorous," said the nurse as she led me into the Linac room.

"I'm going to the ballet after this!" I said, with what I could feel was a stupid grin on my face.

I was a visitor to two very different worlds that day. The final session done, I hopped on the bus back into the city centre, and met husband and children for lunch at a very decent restaurant.

My conflicting images: a hospital waiting room, like all hospital waiting rooms, sick people, their worried relatives, overworked nurses bustling along the corridors, delivering smiles and treatment to the patients, fluorescent lighting…; and then husband, children, bright laughter, excitement, hot, beautiful, nourishing food, zealous waiters, warm lighting, Christmas decorations, and on to the Festival Theatre for a sumptuous performance of *The Nutcracker* in ostentatious surroundings…

And with that change of scene came the end of my cancer journey. It was over. In the past. Done and dusted. Move on.

I Aitken

The After Effects

Moving on is harder than you might think.
Especially so when one's pet cat is then diagnosed with lung cancer, as ours was, and led over the rainbow bridge to that meadow full of mice in the sky – on Christmas Eve.

I'm not blaming the cat for having bad timing.

We adopted her when she was nine, so we never knew her as a kitten; she was an elegant, disdainful, slightly feral old lady. She was eccentric, sometimes surprisingly tolerant, and always a diva. She would accept our affection with pleasure, to some degree; and then quickly decide she'd had enough attention and swipe us with slightly unsheathed claws. I identified with her, to be honest. We were sisters by very different, other-species misters.

A couple of weeks before Christmas, and the end of my own treatment, she stopped eating food, started losing weight. Husband became concerned and took her for a blood test, which showed nothing. But then she grew lethargic, her head hanging down, failing to stand with an arched back when we stroked her. Husband pointed out that her breathing was laboured, and he started timing each painful inhale and exhale. She returned to the vet for a scan, which showed multiple tumours on her lungs.

Steroids briefly returned some perkiness but soon she was disappearing upstairs and burying herself under son's duvet, something she had never done before, albeit son was her favourite member of the family. It was obvious she was preparing to drift away. Though we did the kindest thing, it was hard, and traumatic.

And for a wee while there I was irrationally angry; not just because we had lost our cat but because I felt cancer had won, after all. It was almost as though the universe was saying, don't be smug. Don't relax. There has to be a balance. And despite being a science fangirl, a lover of the explainable, the logical, I also have faith in unknown energies, in nature's unseen, uncharted power. In yin and yang.

But the loss of our cat contributed only the smallest part to the tediously lengthy emotional healing process.

Friends bump into me now (one year after the end of treatment, as I write), and ask, pointedly, "But how are you? Are you all better?" And they nod at me with kind eyes, willing me to be positive.

"Yes, all better now," I say. Sometimes I add that I'm in remission but mostly, these days, I don't. And occasionally I mention the ongoing scars and side effects, but mostly I don't.

Friends want me to be better.

But everyone should know, cancer is not like that. I had no idea, at the time, just how much of a long-term impact it would have. "You have been very calm through all this," husband said at one point near the end of treatment. I mean, that's quite a funny thing for anyone to say to me, because I'm not in the least bit calm. But on this occasion, I knew there was no point getting stressed. I was ill. It was out of my control. I would sit back and let the doctors get on with curing me. And after I was cured – and I was confident I would be – I could get on with life again. Assuming such a cool, positive, objective point of view, I could afford to be calm.

But for a year afterwards I had days of utter fatigue. I would be sailing along, walking the dog, doing the housework, socialising with friends, powering through my days, and then, suddenly… my alarm went off and I couldn't move. My mind was awake but my body refused to stir. On those days, I listened to my body. I had to; my limbs didn't work. I slept for several more hours. I had a slow day.

Other side effects:

1) Menopause. Chemotherapy launched me into premature menopause; there was a 50/50 chance that my periods would return. They haven't. They won't. I guess that, at the grand old age of 44, my body decided I was as close as goddammit to menopausal age anyway, so we might as well stick with it. I'm pretty much okay with this now. More of my friends are catching up, so I don't feel left out. In fact, when I hear talk of hot flushes, I chime in with my veteran opinion, smug with knowledge. I've

been lucky, I think. I haven't had to deal with any of the peri-menopausal trauma*, which sounds an awful lot like puberty. The only real symptom is those hot flushes, which are bearable. Oh, and tissue paper skin, which is wrinkling and crinkling at an alarming rate. "Your hands are much more wrinkly than my friend's mum's," said daughter, in a tone that was probably unjudgemental but I couldn't help feeling was one of disdain. The rosacea that unexpectedly popped up during chemo has not quite disappeared; lurking beneath the surface of my skin, it rears its scarlet head when I am tired or hot or under the influence of red wine.

2) Lymphoedema. As per the previous chapter. I had no idea, really, that lymphoedema would be the result of a full axilla clearance; if it had come under my radar, I certainly paid little attention. This is a condition I will have for the rest of my life, and which has no cure. It will require regular gentle massaging and an offensively unattractive pressure sleeve and glove combo.

3) Plumpness. On my first visit back to the oncologist after treatment had ended, she complimented me on how well I was looking. "You've lost weight!" she said, delightedly. (That's not totally irrelevant, since the steroids do lead to weight gain, so it's pretty achievable to lose that.) "Yes," I said, "apart from the hideous tyre around my belly! What's that about?" And it is a burden I do not enjoy bearing, since it is bulky, and scarred with stretch marks, and oddly imbalanced, thanks to the liposuction endured the year before. "That's the tamoxifen," said Dr B, sweeping aside any blame that could have been apportioned to me. "What?" I said. "The tamoxifen leads to weight gain around the belly," said Dr B. This news both pleased me and pissed me off. It meant that a) the plumpness wasn't my fault, so I wasn't being a greedy cow but that b) there was nothing I could do about it.

4) Physical scarring. There is some, and of course it's all thanks to the treatments and not much to do with the cancer. My hair, which used to be thick and plenty, is thinner, with a marked receding hairline (though this, I have just discovered, is probably down to the tamoxifen). There is

---

* "Peri-menopausal! Isn't it an awful term?!" said a friend. "I hate it."
"It sounds like an American car salesman," I replied. "Hi, I'm Perry Menopausal; if your dream has four wheels, I've got the dream for you."

a permanent and larger than necessary scar where the portacath was in my chest, a scar I occasionally and absent-mindedly rub with my fingers, which is ironic, since just the sight, let alone the touch, of the portacath when it was in made me boak. Most of all, though, is my poor battered boob. After three operations, it is lopsided, the nipple twisted and wonky, looking in an entirely different direction from the one it ought. It looks like it's fallen out with the other boob. Twice now, Mr A has suggested he could do some cosmetic surgery to straighten things up. Twice I have considered it. Though my boob is now nobody's business but mine and my husband's, so nothing to feel self-conscious about, it is still… freakish. Unattractive. But more and more I am seeing it as a battle scar, the proof I was attacked by death and won. Ha! And there was me denying that cancer patients "battle" their illness. Well then, perhaps they do. Perhaps, despite the physical fight being undertaken by the surgeons, there is a battle of sorts engaged in the patient's mind, in their soul, their subconscious, their very will to live. The fight to survive. So. The wonky boob remains, a monument to my victory.

5) Emotional scarring. I didn't think I'd have any. But here we are, one year down the line, and it is a large section of the rich tapestry of my life; not helped – lol – by the writing of this book. I guess it would be unreasonable to expect to be able to get over nine months of treatment. It has especially scarred my husband and children, though they wouldn't say that, even admit it. How difficult it must be to watch a loved one sleep so much, lose all their hair, be constantly carted into hospital to be pumped full of cytotoxins. I had the easy bit! A couple of months after the end of treatment, our local librarian did a wonderful thing and decided to open up a room in the library once a month for a cancer support group, if one could be formed. I heard about it through my hairdresser – I hear about everything through my hairdresser – and went along. It was me and one other patient that first meeting; but we knew this was a brilliant idea, since otherwise patients in our region had to make the journey into the city to visit the albeit wonderful Maggie's Centre. So we spread the word, put up posters, created social media accounts, and since then, every month, there has been a large or small group of cancer patients and their loved ones, joining us to chat about their illness, their fears, their sadness, the weather, what book they're reading, the nuisance of PICC lines… And we

have listened to their stories, provided them with information, and brought them together with a roomful of likeminded people who understand them. Sadly, what has arisen from that group is the sense that they very often feel abandoned by their health professionals, not listened to, sometimes misdiagnosed, left to their own devices. And this, I think, is not only due to the immense pressures on health professionals, but also to the fact that cancer is so pervasive in our society. Half of those born after 1960 will be diagnosed with some form of cancer during their lifetime[78]. It's damn common. I've *seen* the Cancer Centre – it's a conveyor belt of patients, rolling in, being treated, rolling out again. It must be difficult for health professionals to treat so many people like humans, rather than cases. Yet that is what is so important with cancer – it isn't a common cold, it's a frightening illness with so many stigmas around it and an array of bloody violent treatments attached. It's traumatic to go through. Patients do need their hands held, and follow-up calls to make sure they understand and can recover from what happened to them.

Seven months after the end of treatment. I visited Dr B for a check-up and mammogram. It was painful, as always, especially trying to negotiate my wonky boob between the glass plates (are they glass? Can't remember). I think it was at that visit that Dr B blamed the tyre around my belly on tamoxifen. Husband was no longer accompanying me on these appointments, of course. These were run-of-the-mill follow-up sessions, when I had no need of his support.

I can't quite work out what happened next, since the dates in my diary don't seem to add up. Suffice it to say, I was then informed that something had been spotted on the mammogram, and I would need to have a stereotactic biopsy for further investigation. Mmm, biopsies, my favourite.

The deep intake of breath and hoiking back of my shoulders was palpable. *Well*, I thought. *We're going to go through this again. Okay then – let's get on with it.*

Since bloody when have I been so prosaic?

The biopsy took several weeks to organise, since it would need to be done in the NHS hospital, and apparently everyone needed to go through seven levels of bureaucracy first.

Eventually, I got a call from a doctor at the hospital, asking me to go in the next day for the biopsy. "Erm, no, sorry," I said.

"Pardon?" said the doctor.

"I have other plans for tomorrow. You can't really call me up and ask me to drop everything…" I thought I was being reasonable, and I did say all that as politely as possible. The doctor was clearly bamboozled, and insisted that Dr B wanted me to come in. "There isn't another appointment available for three weeks."

"Yes," I said, "but it's taken three weeks to get this appointment, so it's not an emergency. I can wait another three weeks." If that's not being reasonable, I don't know what is. Except that she was obviously looking at my notes, because when this call had ended, she called me back again soon after to offer me an appointment in five days' time.

I learned from the notes only afterwards that what they had spotted on the mammogram looked a lot like DCIS, meaning that either not all the cancer from the first illness had been cleared up, or that a new cancer was baking in my boob oven.

So, five days later, in I trotted to hospital. And then spent 20 minutes or so wandering aimlessly around the hospital corridors trying to locate the stereotactic biopsy department. I was met with quite a lot of blank faces, some helpful and not quite correct directions, and lots of chat about a South Corridor and Link Corridor. I felt like a rat in a maze, and one without a particularly pleasant treat at the end.

Eventually I found the right department, and was settled into a chair by quite the loveliest and kindest nurse, who was gentle, softly-spoken, congenial and solicitous.

The doctor to whom I had spoken on the phone arrived, and explained what would now happen[79]. Ah yes, because this would be like no other biopsy I had experienced: I would be sitting up in front of a machine, my breast held still by glass plates; an x-ray would be taken to make sure I was being drilled in the right place; and then the doctor would perform the actual biopsy, which I didn't watch, for obvious reasons, but which went something like having a small drill plunged into the breast, and the obligatory snap back of a spring. It wasn't entirely pleasant, but it really wasn't as awful as the nurse maybe thought I would think it was. If you follow.

I felt a warm trickle down my stomach and onto my hand, and when I was moved away from the machine and the chair reclined, it turned out to be blood. Which had trickled onto my white jeans. The doctor hastened to give me advice on how to wash blood from white jeans, but I wasn't bothered.

"It'll come out eventually," I shrugged.

A large pad was taped over the hole and I was sent on my way. I met a friend in the city for dinner, and would have forgotten all about the biopsy if it wasn't for the fact that my boob was, again, bruised and sore.

"Oh!" I suddenly said to my mate. "I've just realised it's my wedding anniversary."

A week and a half later I was back in clinic for the results.

"Everything is okay," said Dr B, matter-of-factly. "There is no DCIS, it is just scarring. So, we talked about the Zometa* injections didn't we? We should get you referred for..."

"Umm, it was just scarring?" I said. "On the mammogram? Nothing else?"

"No, nothing at all. It's a shame that you had to go through what you did to confirm that, but obviously it's best that we know for sure."

Of course.

In the midst of my cancer treatment, I wrote a list of things I would like to do and get once the shitstorm was over, a list of things I could dream about[80]:

- Buy a dog
- Buy a motor home
- Visit Venice & Florence. And most of Europe
- Visit Crieff Hydro
- Buy a Jaguar i-Pace
- Get two more tattoos
- Go out for dinner more

Yeah, a couple of those were maybe a bit ambitious, specifically the Jaguar and motorhome, but last year we bought a dog, visited Venice

---

* Zometa – a brand name for zoledronic acid, the next phase of treatment, which will be delivered via infusion into the vein twice a year, and is intended to prevent breast cancer spreading to the bones, and also to prevent calcium loss and osteoporosis[81]

(and some other bits of Europe; also the USA), I had one more tattoo…
Husband would say we've eaten out a lot, too, but I don't think we've
increased the incidence of dining out at all.

What we have done is live. Enjoy living. Spend time together. My daily
walk with the dog on the beach is absolutely the most life-affirming thing I
have ever done – the light is different every day, the sea is an unknown and
ever-changing force; some days, when it's stormy and I'm wrapped up in
warm waterproofs, the dog and I have the beach to ourselves. I look across
the firth and watch the sunlight reflecting off distant windows, and making
even greener the hills beyond. I watch the sea faithfully echo the colour of
the skies above. My favourite shade is a steel grey so iridescent it makes
the sea one vast mirror.

Epilogue

Was it my fault? I did ask myself this pretty often. Was it somehow karma for all the times I've behaved like a little shit? And boy, have I behaved like a little shit. I've been temperamental, and emotional, selfish, thoughtless, uncaring, rude, unprofessional… Sometimes all at once.

But that's quite a dangerous road to go down – to believe that karma really does exist, and it's only the naughty people who are punished by illness. Which is of course a nonsense.

As for lifestyle… I thought that breast cancer was genetic. Or bad luck. I certainly thought mine was both. But recently I did a bit more digging – not much, actually, it doesn't take much effort to uncover the theories behind the causes of cancer.

"A person's risk of developing cancer depends on many factors, including age, genetics, and exposure to risk factors (including some potentially avoidable lifestyle factors)," says Cancer Research UK[82]. "Eight percent of breast cancer cases in the UK are caused by alcohol drinking."

Ah, well there you are then. I'm not obese, I did breastfeed my babies, I'm not post-menopausal (I wasn't even peri-menopausal when I first fell ill)… But alcohol? I have always, since university, drank too much alcohol. Way more than the recommended intake for men, let alone women. I'm not an alcoholic, but I do tend to lean on alcohol to have fun. To relax. To forget.

Maybe… possibly… my cancer was because of my lifestyle choices.

Okay, so the Japanese doctor, the genetic counselling service and my oncologist had all taken a look at my family history and concluded that, despite the fact my BRCA test was negative, my cancer was, in all likelihood, hereditary.

But still. I can't have helped things. I was genetically predisposed to having breast cancer, but maybe I could have held it off if I had just cut down the alcohol.

Dear me.

Is this avenue of thought healthy or necessary?

Do other cancer patients blame themselves? Ask themselves questions about how they've lived their life, look back over their past, raking through the choices made? It turns out that yes, they do. The online forums are full of women who, having survived breast cancer, have entirely changed their lifestyle, in the (subconscious) belief that it was their fault for getting the illness in the first place. They are losing weight, eating healthily, exercising.

Which is a good thing, of course. But what happens if they do get ill again? Because we can be as healthy as we like, but we all die in the end. I like fruit cake, and alcohol, and Chinese takeaway… If I gave all those up and became slender, fit and healthy, I'd be miserable.

Just kidding. A bit.

My post-cancer epiphany was not restricted to thoughts of self-care and a healthy lifestyle.

Husband bought a book – *Ikigai: the Japanese Secret to a Long and Happy Life*[83]. Since our trip to Eastern Asia, I was a fan of pretty much all things Japanese (not all, obviously. Some things are a bit unsavoury). But I hadn't heard of the philosophy of *ikigai*[84] – roughly translated as "reason for being". It was a revelation. The philosophy goes something like *plate iii*.

To achieve some sort of equilibrium in existence, we should strive to do what makes us happy, what we are good at, what the world needs and, obviously in a capitalist society, what we can get paid for. Not everyone can attain this balance – the world isn't that fair. But it struck me that if we think in these terms, we could reach some sort of meaning, a basic happiness.

Rather than do what people say matters, we should do what matters to us. And if we can make the shift from doing to being, we will find more sense in our lives, more beauty and connection.

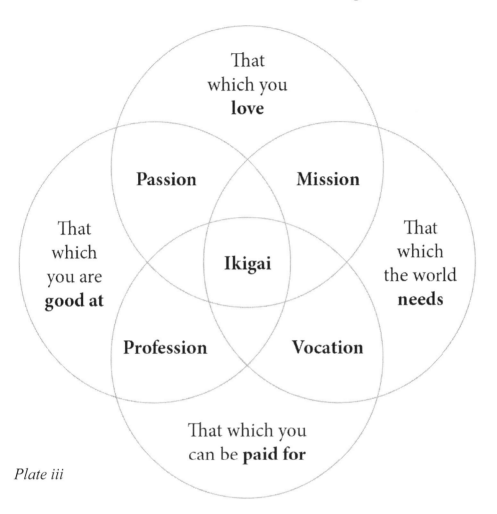

That
which you
love

Passion   **Mission**

That
which
you are
good at

Ikigai

That
which
the world
needs

Profession   **Vocation**

That which you
can be **paid for**

Plate iii

It's not all hippy nonsense, honestly. I'm a natural born cynic. But when I was ill, I lost a lot of my rage, my desire to fight. Life's too short for anger and violence.

That's not to say one can't be passionate, of course not. I'm the first one to eff and blind at drivers who don't indicate. There is still so much to fight for in this post-Brexit, Trump-inflicted world. But rather than be motivated by fury at political injustice, I want to be energised by what can be, what should be, what everyone deserves to enjoy: peace, shelter, warmth, food, love.

What is the moral of this story?

That humans suffer, are pained, and encounter obstacles – but we are all suffused with an absolute instinct to survive. We take those injuries and we make them a part of us, the scars building blocks for our characters. We make pearls from the grit.

ENDNOTES

1 go-nihon-go.travel.blog
2 gov.uk/foreign-travel-advice/japan/entry-requirements
3 en.wikipedia.org/wiki/Japanese_writing_system
4 runforthecure.org/en/
5 en.wikipedia.org/wiki/Prefectures_of_Japan
6 tokyo-park.or.jp/park/format/index039.html
7 tokyo-dome.co.jp/en/tourists/
8 en.m.wikipedia.org/wiki/Junji_Takada
9 en.wikipedia.org/wiki/Romanization_of_Japanese
10 en.wikipedia.org/wiki/BRCA_mutation
11 macmillan.org.uk/information-and-support/breast-cancer/dcis/understanding-cancer/what-is-dcis.html
12 nhs.uk/conditions/Hydrocephalus/
13 A more comprehensive description of the purpose, role and behaviour of cerebrospinal fluid can be found at en.wikipedia.org/wiki/Cerebrospinal_fluid
14 en.wikipedia.org/wiki/Cerebral_shunt
15 skincancer.org/skin-cancer-information/merkel
16 hindawi.com/journals/bmri/2014/986829/
17 en.wikipedia.org/wiki/Archibald_McIndoe
18 breastcancercare.org.uk/information-support/have-i-got-breast-cancer/benign-breast-conditions/intraductal-papilloma
19 nice.org.uk/about
20 breastcancercare.org.uk/sites/default/files/publications/pdf/intraductal-papilloma-2015.pdf
21 nhs.uk/conditions/predictive-genetic-tests-cancer/
22 siddharthamukherjee.com/the-emperor-of-all-maladies/
23 breastcancercare.org.uk/information-support/have-i-got-breast-cancer/benign-breast-conditions/fibroadenoma
24 nursingtimes.net/Journals/2013/03/15/m/w/w/050322The-NPSA-recommendations-to-promote-correct-site-surgery.pdf
25 en.wikipedia.org/wiki/Shell_shock
26 Medical Muses: Hysteria in Nineteenth-century Paris by Asti Hustvedt
27 Handbook of PTSD, First Edition: Science and Practice edited by Matthew J. Friedman, Terence M. Keane, Patricia A. Resick
28 ptsd.va.gov/professional/PTSD-overview/ptsd-overview.asp
29 nhs.uk/conditions/post-traumatic-stress-disorder-ptsd/symptoms/
30 en.wikipedia.org/wiki/Fight-or-flight_response
31 nhs.uk/conditions/cognitive-behavioural-therapy-cbt/
32 macmillan.org.uk/information-and-support/breast-cancer/dcis/understanding-cancer/what-is-dcis.html
33 breastcancercare.org.uk/oncotype-dx
34 cancerresearchuk.org/about-cancer/what-is-cancer/how-cancer-can-spread?utm_source=affiliate_window&utm_medium=affiliate&utm_name=online_retail&utm_content=www.skimlinks.com&dclid=CPi02bui_
35 huffingtonpost.co.uk/entry/hospital-fart-fire_us_5818b2c4e4b0990edc3388cf
36 en.wikipedia.org/wiki/Ileus
37 goodhousekeeping.com/health/diet-nutrition/a16627/caffeine-content-breakdown-beverages/
38 maggiescentres.org/our-centres/

maggies-edinburgh/
39 lookgoodfeelbetter.co.uk
40 cancerresearchuk.org/about-cancer/
cancer-in-general/tests/bone-scan
41 cancerresearchuk.org/about-cancer/
cancer-in-general/treatment/
chemotherapy/how-you-have/into-your-
vein/portacath
42 nhs.uk/conditions/electrocardiogram/
43 nhs.uk/conditions/echocardiogram/
44 breastcancercare.org.uk/about-us/news-
personal-stories/cold-caps-do-they-work
45 nhs.uk/conditions/stress-
anxietydepression/mindfulness/#what-
ismindfulness
46 en.m.wikipedia.org/wiki/Pegfilgrastim
47 macmillan.org.uk/information-
andsupport/coping/side-effects-
andsymptoms/other-side-effects/
peripheral-neuropathy.html
48 go-nihon-go.travel.blog/2017/03/15/
knock-knock-whos-there-doctor/
49 nhs.uk/conditions/Oedema/
50 scottishpoetrylibrary.org.uk/poetry/
poets/jackie-kay
51 youtube.com/watch?v=Ju0BaLIIJvM
52 youtube.com/watch?v=zO_
YowFKpx4&t=335s
53 youtube.com/user/MoreZoella
54 youtube.com/user/Sprinkleofglitter
55 undiscoveredscotland.co.uk/livingston/
bangour/
56 en.wikipedia.org/wiki/2017_
Westminster_attack
57 en.wikipedia.org/wiki/Manchester_
Arena_bombing
58 en.wikipedia.org/wiki/2017_London_
Bridge_attack
59 en.wikipedia.org/wiki/Grenfell_Tower_
fire
60 macmillan.org.uk/information-and-
support/treating/hormonal-therapies/
individual-hormonal-therapies/
tamoxifen.html
61 macmillan.org.uk/information-and-
support/treating/hormonal-therapies/
individual-hormonal-therapies/
goserelinbreast-cancer.html
62 womensmentalhealth.org/posts/
citalopram-celexa-effective-for-
treatinghot-flashes/
63 alnwickcastle.com
64 bbc.com/future/story/20170210-a-test-
can-identify-supertaskers-but-only-a-
few-pass-it
65 nhs.uk/conditions/amyloidosis/
66 www.sciencealert.com/pregnancy-baby-
brain-mumnesia-cognitive-function-
meta-analysis – this article avers
that mumnesia is something women
experience only while pregnant. Frankly,
I feel I never recovered even after giving
birth.
67 macmillan.org.uk/information-
andsupport/coping/side-effects-and-
symptoms/other-side-effects/chemo-
brain.html
68 everydayhealth.com/menopause/brain-
fog.aspx
69 cancerresearchuk.org/about-cancer/
breastcancer/treatment/surgery/remove-
lymph-nodes
70 macmillan.org.uk/information-
and-support/treating/radiotherapy/
radiotherapy-explained/planning-
yourtreatment.html#5824
71 breastcancercare.org.uk/information-
support/facing-breast-cancer/going-
through-breast-cancer-treatment/
radiotherapy-primary
72 nhs.uk/conditions/radiotherapy/
sideeffects/
73 collinsdictionary.com/dictionary/
english/psychosomatic
74 nhs.uk/conditions/Lymphoedema/
75 macmillan.org.uk/information-and-

support/coping/complementary-
therapies/complementary-therapies-
explained/massage-therapies.html

76 madeforlife.org

77 scienceblog.cancerresearchuk.
org/2017/07/12/an-introduction-to-
radiotherapy-what-is-it-how-does-it-
work-and-whats-it-for/

78 cancerresearchuk.org/health-
professional/cancer-statistics-for-the-
uk#heading-Zero

79 breastcancercare.org.uk/information-
support/have-i-got-breast-cancer/
referral-breast-clinic/mammograms-
breast-scans/fine-needle-
aspiration#core%20biopsy

80 thecword2017.wordpress.
com/2017/07/05/too-hot-to-handle/

81 macmillan.org.uk/information-and-
support/treating/supportive-and-other-
treatments/bisphosphonates/zoledronic-
acid.html#20126

82 cancerresearchuk.org/health-
professional/cancer-statistics/statistics-
by-cancer-type/breast-cancer#heading-
Four

83 goodreads.com/book/show/33357041-
ikigai

84 en.wikipedia.org/wiki/Ikigai

I Aitken

ACKNOWLEDGEMENTS

Thanks in this section would normally be for those who have supported the publication of the book – in my case it's also for all those who supported me through my illness and literally enabled this book's existence.

So, thanks to Kiei Kim of the Run For The Cure Foundation, Tokyo; Doctors Kajiura and Fukatsu at St Luke's International Hospital, Tokyo; my incredible healthcare team of consultant, oncologist, chemo nurses, surgeons and anaesthetists at Spire Murrayfield Hospital, Edinburgh; the radiotherapy nurses at Western General Hospital, Edinburgh; and my GPs and the receptionists at North Berwick Health Centre. All these medical folk are superstars.

Shout out to the amazing folk at Maggie's Centre – they provide such an essential service, and would be very grateful for your donations – visit maggiescentres.org/how-you-can-help/ways-give/ And while you're at it, maybe you could think about supporting Cancer Research UK via cancerresearchuk.org/get-involved/donate and Macmillan Cancer Support via macmillan.org.uk/donate

Thank you to librarian Jennifer for providing a room, tea, coffee and biscuits for the cancer support group.

Thanks, too, to my incredible community of friends, neighbours and acquaintances, for their meals and moral support, good wishes and safety net of concern, but especially to boob cake lady Sandra for being a brilliant baker; to Mairi for her physio; and Bevs 1 & 2, Jess, photographer Emma Martin and schoolfriend Chris for going above and beyond.

Thank you to Caroline and Claire for telling me to stop calling my writing a hobby; without them, this book wouldn't have appeared as soon as it did.

Thank you to the readers of this book's proofs: Annemarie, Susan and especially the incredibly kind Carys Bray, who provided her time and expertise despite having her own publishing deadline to meet.

Massive, huge thanks to Cherry for travelling so far so frequently to do all the mum stuff and be amazing; to Roy for encouraging her; and to Thomas & Scarlett for being so amusing.

Thanks to my brave, kind, beautiful Rab & Maia.

And endless thanks to Michael, for your unbelievable strength, support, courage and kindness. I love you.

ABOUT THE AUTHOR

Isla's long and varied career has included a stint working as sub editor on titles including *Dentistry Monthly* magazine, a brief period as an ardent environmental campaigner, and an even briefer stint as a wannabe politician. She has also published two short stories, The Mill Pond and The Dark Surrounds.

Printed in Great Britain
by Amazon